ESCAPE FROM TAIWAN

Legacy of Oppression

By

CHIUFANG HWANG, M.D.

Escape From Taiwan: Legacy of Oppression, Published January, 2019
Editorial and proofreading services: Kathleen A. Tracy, Karen Grennan
Interior layout and cover design: Howard Johnson
Photo credits:
Front cover: Pixabay-CC0 Creative Commons
Title Page and Chapter Openers: Dragon Silo; Designed by Freepik
All photographs are the sole owner of the author, Chiufang Hwang, M.D.

SDP Publishing

Published by SDP Publishing, an imprint of SDP Publishing Solutions, LLC.

To obtain permission(s) to use material from this work, please submit a written request to:

SDP Publishing
Permissions Department
PO Box 26, East Bridgewater, MA 02333
or email your request to info@SDPPublishing.com.

ISBN-13 (print): 978-1-7321115-9-2
e-ISBN-13 (ebook): 978-1-7327933-2-3

Library of Congress Control Number: 2018964675

Printed in the United States of America

TABLE OF CONTENTS

PREFACE 5

INTRODUCTION...9

1 THE BEAUTIFUL ISLAND..................................14

2 OCCUPATION... 22

3 EARLY LIFE IN AMERICA 34

4 CULTURE SHOCK 44

5 PAT 58

6 ANNIE 74

7 MARY 90

8 WHAT'S LOVE GOT TO DO WITH IT?........... 106

9 DOC 121

10 YOU CAN GO BACK AGAIN,
BUT IT'S NOT HOME 135

EPILOGUE: LOOKING FORWARD 150

BIBLIOGRAPHY.. 155

PREFACE

The United States is a country of immigrants. Unless you're Native American, your family came here across some ocean at some point during the last few hundred years. The European cultures have been well documented, from the Pilgrims escaping religious persecution to the Irish fleeing the potato famine. But not much has been written about the Asian immigrant experience in general or the Taiwanese community in particular.

The first incarnation of this book was a planned scholarly psychological case study of American-raised daughters of Taiwanese immigrants. But upon reflection, I realized presenting the experience I lived first-hand in a dispassionate, academic presentation would do the story I wanted to tell—not to mention the readers—a disservice. I want to tell the story of people, not subjects. I think the more we understand about other ethnicities, cultures, and nationalities, the more empathy we'll have and perhaps the better we can coexist.

Taiwanese people in general and Taiwanese immigrants in particular tend to be very private, insular, and emotionally reserved. It might be a stereotype, but it also happens to be a very real cultural trait. As a rule, no matter how turbulent our lives are, we maintain tranquil appearances. Our parents were raised to be very secretive, even with their closest friends. And that instinct to fly under the radar and not cause waves was borne from an ingrained fear passed down through many generations, the legacy of living under an oppressive regime that ruled with brutality, where vocal dissent could be fatal.

Many Taiwanese who came to the United States in the last half of the twentieth century, still looked over their shoulder, careful to keep their political opinions about the ruling party in Taiwan to themselves, fearful of possible consequences. For those born and bred in the United States I'm sure it sounds paranoid, something out of a John Le Carré spy novel. Usually the biggest threat Americans face for criticizing their current government is an argument during Thanksgiving dinner. But if you think authoritarian powers-that-be aren't dangerous, just consider the number of ex-pat Russian dissidents who have ended up poisoned in the past decades, including the March 4, 2018, attack in England on a former Russian spy, Sergei Skripal, and his daughter with military grade nerve agent.

Taiwan's totalitarian government carried out several suspected hits of their own over the years but they mostly controlled their ex-pats by holding relatives in Taiwan accountable. If you wanted your parents to keep their jobs or didn't want Uncle to disappear, you avoided doing anything that could bring unwanted attention, keeping your political opinions to yourself regardless of where you were in the world.

And we're not talking ancient history here. Martial law did not end in Taiwan until 1987; the first free—and fair—elections took place in 1992; and the first fully democratic presidential election was held in 1996. My parents moved to the United States in the late 1960s so even though I grew up in this country, I was raised by people whose outlook was informed by fear and oppression, and they did their best to instill in me the dangers of speaking out—about anything. My mother especially kept me on a very short leash even when I was in college, not wanting me to have a social life outside their small circle of other Taiwanese families because you never knew who might be spying on you. She clung tightly to all things Taiwan, from the food she cooked to her refusal to learn English to not wanting me to blend in with American kids and dressing me in traditional Chinese styles when I was younger. While it may have been her security blanket and made her feel closer to those she left behind, it made for a lot of childhood confusion and teenage resentment from me.

It wasn't until I was older that I discovered the daughters in the other Taiwanese families I'd grown up around had also all gone through the same emotional and cultural struggle to find their identity, which affected our efforts to assimilate at school, in our neighborhoods, and with our peers when we were younger. It also created conflicts, both internal and familial, as we became adults. Leaving the nest is a rite of passage all teens and young adults go through. It's made more complicated when your parents see your rejection of their Old World customs as not just a rejection of them but of your heritage.

Much to my mother's chagrin, I had an independent streak that was decidedly American. I was also ambitious. There were not enough spies in the world to keep me from going to medical school and being a success. I also made life choices I knew my parents wouldn't approve of—like getting engaged without asking their permission—because I wasn't willing to sublimate my life and goals just to make them happy or abide by quaint customs. It's not that I didn't respect the cultural traditions my parents embraced, but they were designed for a different place and time. They simply didn't apply to my life in Texas. It's a fine line many first-generation children of immigrants constantly walk. I was willing to endure my parents' occasional disappointment for not being traditional enough or dutiful to their wishes. But not all my Taiwanese friends were, so we ended up taking very different paths in life.

But regardless of where we ended up, we were all products of the generations that came before us in our family trees. We may not have lived under Japanese occupation in the 1800s or totalitarian Chinese rule after World War II, but those events shaped the people our grandparents were, who in turn shaped our parents who in turn influenced who we became, either by acquiescence or rebellion. Their legacy is ours by default, but that doesn't mean we can't change the narrative. For Taiwanese immigrants, instead of teaching fear, we can instill hope. Instead of being socially isolated and insular, we can encourage inclusion and show the benefit of diversity. Instead of watching from afar in silence, we can support those in Taiwan who seek to maintain democracy.

The original purpose of this book was to tell the story about the immigrant experience of my people. But I now realize that at its heart it's also about the human experience of figuring out who you are, where you belong, reconciling your parent's past with your own present, and deciding what you want to add to your family's legacy for the generations that follow.

In other words, it's the story of us all.

INTRODUCTION

While frowned on today, scaring children into compliance has probably been a tried and true parental strategy since Cain and Abel were bickering at bedtime. Sometime during the Middle Ages, probably in the Scottish Highlands, misbehaving children were told a monster called the bogeyman would take them away, never to be seen again. The bogeyman would have staying power.

Fast forward several centuries and today it refers to any frightening, faceless threat. For Taiwanese children in the United States, the bogeyman was the Kuomintang, or KMT, the authoritarian political party ruling Taiwan. It was well-known that they had spies everywhere who would report any subversive activity back to the regime and get paid for their patriotism. These reports, true or not, could cause problems for family members still on the island. Many of the spies were Taiwanese students, so my father was always careful when at school.

I grew up hearing about the KMT. While American kids were taught not to talk to strangers, Taiwanese kids were warned against talking to anyone because your neighbor or teacher could be a spy. It was like living under a constant overcast sky, hoping it wouldn't rain. When the storm finally came, it caught us completely off guard.

Looking back, I realize my mother was a bit of a stage mom. And let's face it; I've never been shy about performing, so I didn't mind. Back in Taiwan my mother had worked as an elementary school teacher, and it was common for classes to put on skits. When a holiday was coming up, the teacher would pick a theme and direct a performance that usually included some simple dance steps, costumes, and props.

I made my performing debut when I was five during my graduation from Henley Homes kindergarten. The school had given my mother permission to stage some entertainment. My mother was a capable enough chore-ographer; she had taken some ballet classes at a studio for a while, so she borrowed from that for the dance moves. But she did have a sharp fashion sense. She came from a wealthy family and had been a clothes horse as a young woman before getting married to my father. And she knew how to sew, so my costumes were always Chinese in style. My mother acted out the performance, and I memorized her moves. Soon enough it was showtime.

My classmates were milling about, waiting for the show to start. All of the black kids were formally decked out in three-piece suits and party dresses. The few white kids were wearing everyday clothes. But I really stood out in my improvised ballet costume. I was wearing a white tulle tutu, white tights, a white T-shirt sewn onto the homemade skirt, and white bedroom slippers as ballet shoes.

The kids, their parents, and the teachers gathered to-gether, and my mother started the music from the ballet *Swan Lake*, my cue to strike a pose. Then I launched into the performance. The song was a good five minutes, which feels like a really long time when you're in front of an audience. By yourself. Twirling, waving my arms, and prancing. When the song was (mercifully) over, I bowed to everyone. The applause gave me a thrill, a validation that made me feel both shy and pleased.

After that I started performing a few times a year—on Chinese New Year, during summer get-togethers, in September for the Autumn Moon Festival, and over the Christmas holidays.

I was a six-year-old second-grader when I first danced for the Chinese Student Association on Chinese New Year at the University of South Carolina in Columbia, where my father was in a doctorate program. A bunch of students rented a place for a potluck celebration. That night there was a jovial atmosphere, and eventually it was time for my performance. As usual, it was only me. The other kids were off playing in another room. To celebrate the holiday I did the plate dance, which is exactly what it sounds like. You dance around waving plates in the air. Or in my case paper plates wrapped in tin foil to make them shiny under the lights as I waved them around. I was costumed in a lavender nightgown decorated with sequins to make it festive and a floral headband. My mother had added just a touch of makeup: a dusting of face powder, some eyeliner to make my eyes look bigger, her red lipstick on my lips, and a little rubbed on my cheeks. In Chinese culture the color red is believed to bring good luck, so the lipstick represented good fortune for the new year.

People watched politely although I'm sure the college students in attendance couldn't have cared less about a little kid prancing around on stage doing a folk dance. When my performance was over, everyone watching applauded, I took a bow, then ran off to join the other children. It was a good evening all around, getting the new year off to a good start.

That optimism lasted a couple of days until we got

an anonymous letter in the mail, written in Chinese. My mother looked stricken and read it out loud.

> *How dare you put bright-red lipstick on such a young child? She looked like a cocktail lady at the bar in a nightclub. That was something that a sleazy lady would wear. Such red lipstick on a young child is not appropriate. What are you trying to do to your daughter? She looks like a tramp.*

I'd later learn that was code for a prostitute, which was a bit harsh considering I was six.

When my mother put the letter down her hands were shaking, and she kept saying, "Oh, my goodness."

The upshot of the letter was that having me perform in makeup somehow made Taiwan look bad. It was too showy, in bad taste, and not in keeping with the behavior "nationalists" needed to show.

I remember my parents reading the letter over and over. My father's eventual response was to tell my mother to stop having me perform because it drew unwanted attention to our family. In the end my mother ignored my father's directive. I performed a few more times on special occasions, and my mother continued to slather on ever-thicker stage makeup.

My response to the letter was surprise; I couldn't believe I was important enough for a spy to put me in report. It meant I probably had an official file in some regime office back in Taiwan. A six-year-old who lived halfway around the world. That was both surreal and terrifying because like many Taiwanese children, I'd been indoctrinated to fear what the Kuomintang might do. The bogeyman was real and living in Columbia, South Carolina.

It wouldn't be until I was older that I would understand how it was that Taiwan came to be at the mercy of a merciless regime that forced its people to spy on one another and made speaking your opinion—even if you were thousands of miles away from the island—a potentially fatal act of defiance. Taiwan's history of occupation had cultivated a fertile environment for fear, distrust, and betrayal.

THE BEAUTIFUL ISLAND

We hold these truths to be self-evident, that all men are created equal, that they are endowed by their Creator with certain unalienable rights, that among these are life, liberty, and the pursuit of happiness. That to secure these rights, governments are instituted among men, deriving their just powers from the consent of the governed.

— DECLARATION OF INDEPENDENCE

The Revolutionary War didn't just turn thirteen colonies into a nation; it also cemented the American identity, which was based on independent thought, personal freedom, and self-rule. Americans know that if they don't like the president, senators, or congressmen representing them, they can vote in new people every four, six, or two years respectively. I think many Americans take this ability for granted and don't appreciate how that power informs their very way of life.

For most of Taiwan's history over the past five hundred years, its people have not had much say in their country's future or how it's governed. They did not grow up assured freedom of thought and speech were their inalienable rights. They were subjugated or occupied or controlled by any number of foreign countries, with true independence and self-determination elusive.

For many years Taiwan was known as Formosa in Western countries like the United States and Britain. Lore has it that name came from sixteenth-century Portuguese explorers, who were the first known Europeans to reach the island in 1544 and dubbed it *Ilha Hermosa*, which means beautiful island. As Renaissance explorers had a habit of doing, they summarily staked claim to the island on behalf of their mother country and established a colony named Formosa in northern Taiwan in 1626. The interest went beyond natural beauty; the Europeans were looking for resources such as gold, minerals, and spices.

While Taiwan may have been new, exotic, and un-developed to the Portuguese, the island had been home to several indigenous tribes of hunters and later traders for five thousand years who were of Austronesian descent, meaning they were in the same family tree as the indig-enous tribes in Malaysia and the Philippines. They were not ethnic Chinese.

But a hundred years before the Europeans arrived, Chinese from the mainland began crossing the Taiwan Strait in the sixteenth century. They arrived bringing farming tools, clothing, jewelry, and other items to trade for deerskin, deer meat, gold ore, sulfur, and other items Taiwan had to offer. These Chinese were largely made up of fishermen, explorers, and business people, many fleeing the mainland which was going through political turmoil at the end of the Ming dynasty. Most came and went, but a small number of them stayed behind in Taiwan.

In the 1620s the Dutch and Spanish joined the party. The Dutch came looking for gold while the Spanish, with help from one of the indigenous tribes, located sulfur, the main ingredient in gunpowder, in one of the mountain ranges. Also, both countries used Taiwan as a base of operations to establish global trade—and piracy. But these Europeans did not intend to occupy Taiwan and build permanent settlements. So when the locals rose up and rebelled at the foreigners' presence, they withdrew completely.

But before leaving the Dutch had encouraged Chinese from the mainland to immigrate to Taiwan, which helped drive a large wave of immigration from China during the early Qing Dynasty.[1] Some of the influx was prompted by a mini gold rush after gold was found in Eastern Taiwan, but mostly it was people looking for space and a place to start over, away from overcrowding and scarce land on the mainland. To support their presence on the island, the Dutch advertised in Fujian that there was available agricultural land in Taiwan. Anyone willing to relocate to the island was offered land and protection in exchange for the payment of taxes.

Just as the native Indian tribes of North America found their cultures overrun, assimilated, or eliminated by British and other European colonists, the indigenous Taiwanese tribes would soon get elbowed aside by these Chinese colonists who were mostly from Fujian and primarily spoke Hokkien, a dialect of Mandarin.

[1] As an aside for any history wonks, the Qing was China's last imperial dynasty before the Republic of China was established. The Qing ruled from 1644 to 1912, and for much of that time, China was quite prosperous and fairly peaceful.

And just as Americans developed American English, as opposed to British English, over the years, the immigrants from China who settled in Taiwan developed a dialect of Mandarin that was uniquely their own: Taiwanese Hokkien, which is now considered the Taiwanese language and is spoken natively by about 70 percent of the island's population. And the descendants of that wave of Chinese immigrants from southern Fujian are called the Hoklo people, who today consider themselves Taiwanese, not Chinese, even though they share the same ethnicity. China has never acknowledged the difference.

The Dutch eventually left the island in 1662. After the Manchus overthrew the Ming Dynasty on the Chinese mainland and started the Qing Dynasty, a rebel Ming loyalist—and pirate—named Koxinga showed up in Taiwan with twenty-five thousand soldiers in 1661 and drove out the Dutch, who had no interest in fighting over the island. Koxinga established his own anti-Qing government and his soldiers, along with some Ming loyalist refugees from Fujian, settled in. Koxinga died not long after the Dutch left, but his son kept Taiwan an anti-Qing stronghold for the next twenty years. But he died in 1681, and two years later the Qing leader sent a fleet to invade Taiwan and after a brief skirmish, got it back under mainland China control. During those decades after the Dutch left, many of the indigenous tribes (aborigines) retreated to the mountains where many remain to this day.

Anyway, for a couple hundred years, the Taiwanese went about their business, largely removed from the political happenings on the mainland, forging a separate identity. And then the first Sino-Japanese War between Japan and the Qing Dynasty happened. Basically the two countries were fighting over who would get to be Korea's

BFF and determine the future of that country. It was a short conflict, lasting from July 1894 to April 1895. Japan, which had embraced the Industrial Revolution and all the then-new technology that came with it, was a modern nation with a modern military, and its Navy overwhelmed its Chinese opponents rather handily. The peace treaty China signed gave Japan control over various islands off China's coast including Taiwan.

The Taiwanese were not happy at the thought of becoming a Japanese colony, and they rebelled by establishing the Republic of Formosa. Their attempt at independence ended five months later after twelve thousand Japanese troops crushed the rebels and captured the upstart republic's capital, Tainan. Reports from the time noted that the Taiwanese tried to fight off Japan's modern army with outdated weapons including bamboo spears. Under Japan rule the island was called Formosa, and it was occupied for the next fifty years, although not many Japanese nationals moved to the island.

In truth, Taiwan thrived during that time. Japan developed Taiwan's economy and raised the standard of living for most of the people. Many Taiwanese adopted Japanese names and practiced Shinto. But after its defeat in World War II, Japan relinquished control of Taiwan, and the government of the Republic of China, led by Chiang Kai-shek's Chinese Nationalist Party, the Kuomintang (KMT), re-established Chinese control over the island and changed its name back to Taiwan.

While World War II was coming to a close, the Chinese Civil War was gearing up, and fighting started in 1946. On one side was the KMT, on the other was the Chinese Communist Party led by Mao Zedong. While the civil war raged, the Taiwanese stewed in resentment over the KMT, who they saw as corrupt, seizing private property without cause. And the island's economy was floundering under their control. Then in early 1947 their worst fears about the KMT and the mainlanders who came over with them were realized.

On February 27, agents from the Tobacco Monopoly Bureau in Taipei confiscated a cigarette vendor's illegal cigarettes along with her money. While attempting to arrest her, they beat her over the head with a pistol. A large crowd of horrified and angry citizens surrounded the agents, prompting one of them to open fire on the crowd, killing one person.

News of the incident spread rapidly and led to mass protests the next day, February 28. A group of two thousand citizens gathered and marched on the Tobacco Monopoly Bureau. They demanded that the agent who killed the citizen be executed and that the bureau's director resign. Elsewhere, an angry mob of citizens beat two tobacco agents to death.

Another large crowd of Taiwanese gathered outside of the governor-general's office in protest over the heavy-handed tactics of the Tobacco Bureau. With no warning, the KMT opened fire on the protesters, killing several. This spawned protests all across Taiwan that targeted government offices and mainland Chinese transplants. Taiwanese protesters overtook most of the cities and towns.

The civil unrest prompted a government committee to investigate the cigarette vendor affair. But already the military was patrolling Taipei, killing people indiscriminately. In early March the committee—comprised of students, legislators, and other professionals who represented the people—proposed thirty-two governmental reforms designed to democratize Taiwan, including having local Taiwanese in government office, providing freedom of speech, a free press, and guaranteeing the rights of aboriginals. It was Taiwan's own version of the Declaration of Independence.

The KMT's response was swift. The next day reinforcements arrived from the Mainland to crack down on any and all dissent in Taiwan. Soldiers fired upon innocent, unarmed civilians in an attempt to instill fear in the people as a way to restore order. Soldiers executed groups of people, raped women, and beheaded people for the shock value. Students who helped to maintain order in the streets during the rioting were tricked into turning themselves in and were then imprisoned or executed.

After what became known as 228 (for February 28), the ROC constitution was suspended, and Taiwan was placed under martial law and officially stayed that way until 1987. The 228 massacre also marked the beginning of the White Terror, designed to eliminate all political opposition. So even after the uprising was officially over, many people, especially dissidents and academics, started to disappear and were never heard from again. Tens of thousands of other Taiwanese went missing or were imprisoned. The KMT was careful to leave no paper trace of their actions, destroying government documents in a massive cover-up. Estimates of the casualties at the hands of the KMT range from 18,000 to twenty-eight thousand killed or disappeared.

力

Mao's forces won the civil war in 1949, so Chiang Kai-shek and his KMT-led forces made Taiwan their permanent headquarters and base of operations while trying to come up with Plan B to fight Mao's new People's Republic of

China (PRC) government on the mainland. At the same time, Chairman Mao, as he liked to be called, intended to "liberate" Taiwan from the KMT through military force. That never happened because of the Korean War, which started in 1950.

Determined to stop the spread of communism throughout Asia, the United States sent the Navy's Seventh Fleet to patrol the Taiwan Strait to protect the island from invasion. It wasn't so much that America was thrilled with Chiang; it was more he was a better option than communist Mao. The lesser of two evils.

America's naval presence forced Mao's government to delay its invasion plan for Taiwan. The United States also supported the Republic of China's regime on Taiwan holding China's seat in the United Nations. The United States also offered Taiwan aid, which helped the KMT government modernize the economy, which was good, as well as solidify its control over the island, which wasn't so good from the average Taiwanese's perspective. The KMT were hated as much as they were feared, the memory of 228 still festering. That date has as much of an emotional impact for Taiwanese as the attack on Pearl Harbor or 9/11 has for Americans. And the remembrance of the brutality displayed by the KMT still serves as a driving force for true Taiwanese independence.

While Chiang's government started allowing local elections in the 1950s, the central government remained firmly under authoritarian, one-party rule by the KMT for the next several decades. And if you wanted a chance at the best jobs and financial security, you had to join the KMT political party. That was the reason my father and so many others left Taiwan for America, even if it could mean never going back to their homeland again.

2

OCCUPATION

My grandparents grew up under Japanese occupation. My parents grew up during the White Terror period. I think my grandparents had the better situation. Although Japan forcefully suppressed any political and social dissent, made Japanese the official language, and restricted personal freedoms, Japan was mostly interested in Taiwan's economic opportunities, exploiting the island's resources such as minerals and soybean production.

On the other hand Japan helped modernize Taiwan, building roads and railways to improve trade and to make many previously isolated areas, especially along the eastern coast, accessible. Japanese workers also improved the infrastructure with new hospitals, schools, and government buildings. So when the Japanese finally left, Taiwan was much more prosperous than it had ever been.

It wasn't until my family took a trip back to Taiwan when I was ten that I learned anything substantial about my grandparents. Even then, my maternal grandmother's early life remains an enigma. I know she was a midwife—and in fact delivered me in a home birth. Midwives were more highly esteemed than nurses at that time. She was my grandfather's second wife. He had four sons with his first wife before she died. My grandmother's family matched them up even though there was a big age difference. Then together they had five children, including my mother. My grandmother had very little interaction with her stepchildren once they grew up. She claimed they treated her badly after she and my grandfather married. I do know one of my step-cousins became a dentist, and my parents are friendly with him.

A lot of Taiwanese have some Dutch or Portuguese in their lineage because someone in the past married a European, but the maternal side of my family is Han, meaning ethnic Chinese. I know this because I did one of those home DNA kits. I don't know for sure which ancestor came over from Fujian, but I assume it was sometime in the 1800s because that's when Japan ramped up grain production, and my maternal grandfather was a soybean and barley merchant. He did well, so my mother grew up in comfortable surroundings in Tainan. Even after he retired, he remained well known. When I met my husband in the 1980s, his parents and grandparents knew of my grandfather.

There was a big downside to working in grains; it attracted a lot of rats. My mother remembers the family having a lot of cats as well as dogs around when she grew up to keep the house free of rats. But she never considered them pets, just four-legged exterminators.

While my mother grew up in the city, my father was more of a country boy. Many of his relatives were farmers who he says grew practically everything. They also raised chickens. My father's dad was a car mechanic, and his mother was a housewife. They weren't wealthy, but they got by.

My father was the second born; his parents' first child had died in infancy, which was not uncommon. Infant mortality was so high that it became a custom in Asia to have a gathering, called full moon celebrations, when a baby reached one month old because that meant they were more likely to survive into adulthood. It was basically a coming out party for the mother and baby to be formally introduced to friends and extended family. The one-month mark was considered the baby's first birthday, so when they turned one, it was considered their second birthday. That's why "Chinese age" is the chronological age plus one year.

Full moon celebrations are still held today, with relatives and friends bringing gifts to the new baby. Traditional cakes and eggs—dyed red, the color associated with good luck and good fortune—are served. Some people go all out with a catered event at some venue while others have a smaller gathering at home. We held one-month celebrations for both our boys, and they were really enjoyable events.

But after my father was born, to ensure he wouldn't die too, his parents sent him to his maternal grandmother. It was supposed to be a temporary thing, but after his mother got pregnant again, my father ended up staying with his grandmother permanently because by that time grandmother was attached to the kid, she had kept the baby alive past his first birthday, and she was a lonely widow and it gave her purpose. My father, who was very attached to his grandmother, wanted to stay with her, so my father only saw his parents on weekends. He grew up devoted to his grandmother and says he loved her more than his parents. The affection was mutual.

My father thrived on his grandmother's concentrated attention. Of all his siblings, only one besides my father even finished high school, and none of them held professional jobs. The downside was that she spoiled him; he could do no wrong in her eyes, so he grew up believing his needs were more important than anyone else's. Also, not growing up with his parents meant he never developed a warm relationship with his siblings either.

When you look at some members of my father's side of the family, they have shorter statures, are darker skinned, and slightly different eye shape. My DNA test explained why: while I'm 95 percent Chinese, I'm five percent Filipino, which means way back I have an aboriginal relative on my father's side. I'm always amused when I meet people who ask about my ethnic background then tell me I don't look Chinese. What I think it's really is that I don't sound Chinese; I grew up in South Carolina and Texas and have a pronounced Southern accent, which tends to catch people off guard.

My parents were kids when 228 happened, but they still remember it vividly all these decades later, and they grew up with an ever-present uncertainty on who to trust because anybody could be a KMT informer. Considering their backgrounds and temperaments, my parents weren't an obvious match.

When my father was a graduate student, he supported himself by tutoring math. One of his students was a young woman whose close friend—my mother—was in teacher school. They had become friends after taking ballet class together. The young woman's mother decided to play matchmaker and introduced my father to my mother. The marriage was eventually arranged between the families. My father was twenty-six; my mother was only twenty-four.

By 1966 my father had finished his master's degree at National Cheng Kung University and was teaching there as an assistant professor. To get the best opportunities and the best jobs you had to join the Kuomintang. My father didn't want to do that, so instead he applied to several universities in the United States, hoping one would accept him. One did. At the time, the only way you could get out of Taiwan was to be admitted to an American university and prove it. But it was understood that once your education was completed, you were expected to return to Taiwan. Or your family could find their lives complicated. Chiang Kai-shek wanted to avoid a brain drain, and he wanted to keep all Taiwanese under his control as much as possible.

Most of the Taiwanese who came to the United States during that time were graduate students who were anti-Kuomintang. But it was easy to tell which students from Taiwan were KMT; they only spoke Mandarin. The anti-KMT spoke Taiwanese. Language was significant and symbolic of the regime's oppression. Mandarin was the only language taught in schools. During Chiang Kai-shek's rule, the only time you could speak Taiwanese, even among family members, was behind closed doors. If anyone in public heard you speaking anything besides Mandarin, you could be thrown in prison and executed by a firing squad.

力

A little over a year after my parents' wedding I was born. Then five months later my father left for the United States, but my mother and I could not go with him. There was a mandatory two-year wait before the spouse and children could join the student. My father arrived in the United

States in August 1966. My mother and I had to wait until October 1968. By the time we were finally allowed to join my father, my parents hadn't seen each other for twenty-six months, nor had they even corresponded. For one thing, neither of their parents had a phone; most Taiwanese families didn't. If they needed to make a local phone call, they would have to go to a local store. Not that my father would have called Taiwan anyway even if his family or my mother's family had a phone. It was believed that all phone conversations were monitored by operators who were part of the KMT, so anything interpreted as remotely subversive could be reported. Also, all of the letters sent between the United States and Taiwan—usually Aerogrammes—were steamed open and read by the KMT before going in or out of the country.

So once my mother and I arrived, my parents were essentially strangers. And when in Taiwan they had always lived with, and were surrounded by, family. This was the first time they had ever been truly alone together. Add to that my mother going from a comfortable lifestyle to a transient, low-income existence as my father struggled to get his PhD, and it wasn't the stuff of fairy tales.

But they pretty much only had each other, so it was an often tense household. With each failure to complete a doctorate program, the more resentful my mother became. She kept it bottled up where it turned to bitterness, mostly because she had no one to talk to on a daily basis in those early years. For the same reasons my father and mother had never communicated for those two years, neither of my parents felt safe contacting their respective families, especially since my father had no intention of going back. To this day, I wonder how long it took my mother to realize that.

Even though Chiang Kai-shek didn't have the power to tap phones in the United States, old habits die hard, and for many years we never had a phone either. I would tell people it was because we moved so much in pursuit of my father's PhD, but it was more because my parents were worried it would make us more vulnerable to potential spies.

While other kids would talk to friends on weekends or in the evenings, it was radio silence in our house. Did you ever see the old movie *Bye Bye Birdie* with the telephone hour song, all these girls calling each other sharing gossip? That never happened in my house. I didn't even know what a telephone tree was until my kids got into elementary school. That lack of outside communication is something that was alien to the kids I went to school with. Even poor families in the projects had phones by the 1970s. But we didn't get our first phone until after Chiang Kai-shek died when I was in middle school.

As I mentioned, my mother experienced more culture shock than my father. Maybe economic shock is more accurate. My father worked just enough to get by, spending the rest of his time working on one PhD program after another. She'd grown up fairly spoiled and living in poverty-level conditions was not the future she had envisioned for herself. I suspect that's why she felt entitled to government assistance.

Between her downgraded social standing and her concern about KMT-aligned students, she never really enjoyed the freedoms America offered to the fullest, especially during the first seven or so years we were here. She was the most social when we would visit other Taiwanese families. The fathers in all these families were fellow students or professors my father met during his PhD quest.

The families my parents befriended were all staunchly anti-KMT, probably the main reason my mother could relax a bit.

Even though there were not that many Taiwanese families in the area, for some reason South Carolina had several underground anti-KMT groups that we became aware of. I don't know if the same kinds of groups were happening in Taiwan, but they seemed to be blossoming all over the United States.

At the University of South Carolina, there was a little underground group. Years later when we moved to College Station, there was a larger gathering that took place at Sam Houston State University in nearby Huntsville, Texas, every summer around the Fourth of July. I'm sure the timing was no coincidence. Huntsville was chosen because it was centrally located, and the group could rent out the dorms for sleeping accommodations, use the lecture halls for presentations, and hold social events in the big student center. It was in Huntsville every year for many years, and I went with my family to every one of them. To get invited you had to know someone because they wanted to minimize the chance of a potential KMT spy showing up. On the other hand, they didn't really keep that tight of a lid.

A lot of kids my age did their own thing, but I was very intrigued by the group activities. I remember wandering around on campus, and you could just walk into a lecture hall where someone was speaking, which I often did. Now, whether I understood what they were saying is another matter. There is an informal Taiwanese that I understand; this is what my parents spoke at home. But there is also a formal Taiwanese that I barely understood and that's usually what the speakers used. Even though I didn't completely understand what they were talking about, it was very emotional.

They called these large gatherings a camp. When I had first heard about it as a kid, I thought it sounded very exciting because I envisioned canoeing, sleeping outside in a tent ... turns out it was basically a multi-day political retreat that was attended by about five hundred adults and their kids. Okay, not as fun as roasting marshmallows over a roaring campfire but still exciting to be around all those people and listen to the speakers talk about an independent Taiwan, and they would raise money to send to activists in Taiwan. There was a camaraderie that made you feel part of something important.

But it was also scary. We heard stories about how even after Chiang Kai-shek died, the KMT was still very much in control, and elections were rigged. Taiwanese who came to the United States were not allowed to vote, so in the late 1970s everything was still subversive and under the radar. If you were too vocal in the US, the KMT would go and interview your family still in Taiwan as a not-so-subtle threat. We heard they once went to my paternal grandparents' home and asked what my father was still doing in the United States and if he was involved in any anti-government activities. My grandmother was a country lady, she didn't know what her son was doing, but the visit scared her. That was the point: to intimidate the families.

Sometimes they would do more than intimidate. At camp you often saw people who had been injured and maimed because of their political resistance or activities. If someone was crippled and in a wheelchair, you knew they had been victimized. If Chiang Kai-shek thought that you were a troublemaker, either in Taiwan or the United States, or that you were getting too vocal, he would find someone to get rid of you. Often it was accomplished by staging an accident or apparent suicide.

I vividly remember the story of a professor named Wen-chen Chen, an assistant professor at Carnegie-Mellon University in Pittsburgh, Pennsylvania. When he was thirty-one, he had gone back to Taiwan with his wife to visit his ailing mother and have her meet their new baby. As soon as he got off the plane in Taipei, the KMT dragged him away in front of his wife and child. After a thirteen hour interrogation, KMT agents took him to the top of a high-rise then pushed him off the roof. The official story from Taipei was that Dr. Chen had been released unharmed after the interrogation. They claimed Chen admitting to anti-KMT activity in the United States and fearing imprisonment had killed himself. Even if the US State Department doubted the official version of events, it was powerless to do anything.

Chen *had* been very vocal about his anti-Kuomintang views while living in the United States, and the party knew about it. He paid for his beliefs with his life. That story struck a nerve, especially for people like my father and his professor friends. Here was a guy living and working in the United States. He had a wife, an infant, and a professorship at a top university. But hired assassins ended all that.

If the KMT couldn't get to you directly, they would go after your loved ones. Lin Yi-Shing was a vocal critic of Chiang Kai-shek. The KMT set his house on fire when he wasn't home. Lin's mother and children died in the fire.

Lim Gee-Yong was a law professor at National Taiwan University and a prominent anti-KMT activist. Eventually the KMT arrived on his doorstep, but he wasn't home, and his wife was out with one of their daughters. So instead the KMT stabbed his mother to death along with his two other daughters who were home. The surviving daughter ended up moving to the United States but has never spoken publicly about her family tragedy.

My parents and their friends talked a lot about Peng Ming-min at the camps. He's revered as a hero who attempted to overthrow the KMT. Born in Taiwan during the Japanese occupation, Peng went to Japan to study law and political science at the Imperial Tokyo University. In 1945 he left Tokyo to avoid the increasing bombing by the Americans and went to Nagasaki. While there Peng lost his left arm in a bombing raid and later survived the atomic blast that destroyed Nagasaki.

After the war ended he returned to Taiwan. The KMT's violence and oppression both before and after 228 left a lasting impression on Peng. After completing his bachelor's degree at the Law School of National Taiwan University, he went to Canada where he earned a master's degree at McGill University in Canada, then to Paris in 1954 for a doctoral degree in law at the University of Paris. During his studies, Peng's essays on international air law were regularly published, and he was considered a pioneer in the new field of international air law. He returned to Taiwan and at just thirty-four became a professor at the National Taiwan University School of Law.

In 1964 Dr. Peng and his students published *A Manifesto to Save Taiwan* that stated recovering Mainland China was impossible, supported the constitution be amended to guarantee human rights and genuine democracy, and called for Taiwan to participate in the United Nations as a new member and to establish diplomatic relations with other countries as a way of working toward world peace. But before the manifesto could be distributed, Dr. Peng and his students were arrested by the KMT.

One of Peng's friends, a Japanese national, gave Peng his Japanese passport. Peng then disguised himself to look like the passport photo—he wore a fake mustache and added other cosmetic touches—then escaped to Switzerland. His first choice was the United States, but at that time America would not accept Taiwanese refugees seeking political asylum because of their military alliances with the anti-communist Chiang Kai-shek.

The KMT eventually figured out who had helped Peng and set out to capture him, but the Japanese man slipped away under their noses and was safely back in Japan.

Since Peng's exile, many of the proposals in his manifesto have become Taiwanese government policy, which is why Dr. Peng is considered by many to be Taiwan's father of democracy and independence and utterly revered by Taiwanese all over the world. So while many of the stories you heard at the camp were terrifying, there were also stories like those about Dr. Peng that were inspiring and gave hope to people like my father, his friends, and all the camp attendees that one day they would be able to go home again, even if just to visit.

Finally in 1976, a year after Chiang Kai-shek's death, that dream became a reality when my parents took me and my siblings on vacation to Taiwan to visit family I'd not only never met, but basically had never heard of. It would be culture shock in reverse.

EARLY LIFE IN AMERICA

I have no early childhood memories of Taiwan and only brief images of the first year my mother and I were in the United States. The first place we lived was Hempstead, Texas, near Prairie View A&M University, a public, historically black school where my father taught math from 1968 to 1969. We rented a room on a farm. Well, they called it a farm but mostly what I recall was a lot of dense bushes and unmown grass. Our rented quarters were in a row of one-bedroom units at the end of a one-lane dirt road lined on both sides with farm equipment. The owners of the property lived in a nice house. They raised chickens and had a blond daughter named Kim, who became my first American friend. According to my mother, there were snakes in the overgrown brush so she'd carry me to the main house so Kim and I could play together. The way it's been described to me is how I imagine itinerant farmhands live.

Perhaps that's why after a few months we moved to Prairie View, closer to the university and not quite so *Of Mice and Men*. Our new apartment building was an urban fourplex squeezed between a Greyhound depot and an Esso gas station. We weren't there long enough for me to form any lasting memories. For the third time in a year we moved again—I would later know kids with parents in the military who moved less than my family.

Our new zip code was more than a thousand miles east in Rock Hill, South Carolina, where my father had gotten a job teaching math at Friendship College, a well-known traditional black school. We lived on campus in a two-bedroom trailer provided free of charge by the school. Our trailer was parked between the women's dorm and the math department. At least my father didn't have much of a commute to work. We also had to share the trailer with another math teacher, who was from India. Even though our living arrangements were a step away from a youth hostel, it was still an improvement from what we'd had in Texas. During the day I attended Linda's Day Care in Rock Hill, about a ten-minute drive from campus, and at night watched the students passing by or went for walks around the campus with my father.

A year later in 1970 my father was accepted into the PhD program in mathematics at the University of South Carolina, so we moved to Columbia, seventy miles south of Rock Hill. Once again our living conditions improved incrementally. Our new home was in a low-income housing project that looked like Army barracks. There were 110 two-bedroom apartments in Henley Homes, and all qualified residents were assigned units with free electricity and very low rent.

My schooling up to that time did not at all prepare me

for first grade at the well-heeled private school, Timmerman. For one thing, I was still only five. And English was barely my second language since my parents only spoke Taiwanese at home. Everybody else in my class was already reading fluently, while I couldn't even manage *See Spot Run*. I was way behind before I ever stepped foot in the school. My father had enrolled me because starting school early was in fashion among some of the immigrant Chinese families and, more to the point, the first year was free.

Although I struggled with reading, I was good at math, and I didn't feel out of place being the youngest in my class. School was not the source of my worries. I was preoccupied wondering when we were going to pack up and move next. If you're just going to leave, what's the point of making friends? The fear of having to leave behind people I'd grown close to prevented me from trying to make friends at Timmerman.

My brother, Chi-Cheng, was born when I was nearly six years old, and I was so excited to have a living baby doll to play with and no longer be an only child. There's a picture of me next to my mother beside the Plymouth, and a nurse is holding my baby brother. My father brought me to the hospital to take them home, and he took the picture. It was one of my happier days. I had a toy doll my maternal grandmother in Taiwan had shipped to me. She also provided most of my clothing at that time. I loved that doll. But I loved my real, live baby brother exponentially more.

It was Chinese tradition for me to call him Little Brother, and when he learned to talk, he called me Older Sister. I know it sounds overly formal, but our Old-World culture doesn't lean toward the warm and fuzzy. Privacy is also ingrained. Americans will say—often to complete strangers—*Oh, congratulations!* about a visible pregnancy.

But in Asian culture a woman doesn't talk in public about her pregnancy, so my parents were very low-key about it. I'm not sure if it was something you were supposed to be embarrassed about because it meant you'd obviously had sex to get into that condition, or if it was that you dreaded the possibility of a miscarriage and didn't want to jinx it by making a big deal about it.

When he was an infant, I held my baby brother as I would hold a doll, but babies—nor children—were cuddled in my family. As a child I didn't think that was unusual because none of the other Chinese or Taiwanese parents I saw, such as other graduate students, did that with their kids either. It was my normal, so I didn't feel that I emotionally lacked for anything.

Having a new baby meant my parents needed childcare because two weeks after my brother was born, my mother had to go back to work. We couldn't get by on what my father earned, so we needed the money. She was a sewing machine operator at a local undergarment manufacturing company, where she worked from 7:00 a.m. to 5:00 p.m. Basically she made bras, men's briefs, and women's panties. They found my brother a babysitter; the solution for me was to hang with my dad all summer at the University of South Carolina campus. While he was in class, I was in the library. Being extremely small—as an adult I'm barely five feet tall—I'm sure I must have looked like a daycare escapee.

But I kept to myself and out of trouble. I rarely talked when I was young, even when spoken to. Bilingual children are everywhere in the United States' multicultural society, and their mastery is impressive. My command of both English and Taiwanese was mediocre as a younger child. Even though I could speak both languages, I didn't

consider myself bilingual because I knew I wasn't profi-
cient in either. I could not understand even ordinary
Taiwanese news programs and still cannot. My spoken
Taiwanese is conversational, not formal, and it's limited
to humdrum words and phrases. In a Taiwanese church I
couldn't grasp the main idea of the sermon or decipher the
hymns. At those political camps, I could figure out the gist
of the speech but not the specifics. My English was limited
to what I picked up at school, from some babysitters, and
from the street kids who were my companions. In retrospect, I understood English better than I felt I could speak
it. But since my mother made no effort to learn English, it
made it that much more difficult for me to become comfortable speaking it.

In April 1975 my little sister was born. She stole
all our hearts. Mingfang was the cutest, most adorable
baby girl ever. Our family called her Cute Little One in
Taiwanese. We never called her Mingfang or Little Sister.
And no, it didn't pass unnoticed that I was never given an
adorable nickname.

Almost all parents devote a lot of thought to
naming their children. But Taiwanese parents almost
make a science out of it because there is nearly always
meaning behind it. Take my kids. Barrington was so
named because he was conceived while we were living
in Barrington Plaza high-rise apartments in West Los
Angeles. We named our other son Abraham because he
was born after we moved from Los Angeles to Texas.
My husband liked the name Abraham because in the
Bible, Abraham left his home willingly to follow God's
command. He thought our move from Los Angeles for
Texas also involved an element of faith and named our
son Abraham to commemorate that.

The same kind of thought went into my name. I was the only foreign-born child in my family, born in Taiwan during the dazzling springtime. At that time of year, all the fragrant flowers—pink cherry blossoms, scarlet rhododendrons, white calla lilies—are in full bloom. In Mandarin, the phonetic pronunciation of the name my parents gave me is *JO faun* and means *forever fragrant* or *long-lasting fragrance.*

My parents told me that they'd wanted a baby before my father left for the United States. Naming a first-born child is a careful process, and both sets of grandparents had to approve my name. Ironically, I didn't look like a vibrant flower; I was a sickly child, often dizzy, very thin.

When my mother and I left Taiwan in 1968 to join my father, the immigration official spelled my name in English as Chiufang, and that was how I got my Americanized name. The transliteration of a name depended solely on what immigration clerk looked at your Chinese name. If we had been in a different line, I might have gone through life with a different name.

The Taiwanese phonetic pronunciation of my name differs from the Mandarin version—remember, the KMT forbade the use of Taiwanese and demanded everyone speak Mandarin—so at home I was *Hong Eh.* And I was spoken to as *ah Hong.* All Taiwanese names are prefaced by *ah*, which doesn't mean anything; it's just what Taiwanese speakers say before any name. Hong means very fragrant.

My brother's name, Chi-Cheng, means *extremely sincere*, and my sister's name, Mingfang, very similar to mine, means nighttime fragrance. Ming means moon, which designates nighttime; she was born at night. Chinese people don't have middle names, so fang is part of her name; as in my name, it means very fragrant. Our parents had a few names picked out in advance, and the timing of her birth guided their choice.

Unlike formal names, Chinese nicknames are given naturally and without much thought, and in some ways, they are more telling than formal first names.

My brother, Chi-Cheng, always went by Little Brother in our family. In a Chinese family, with several children of each sex, the children would be called Oldest Sister (or Brother), Second Sister, Third Sister, and on down to Youngest Sister.

Being the oldest child is a big deal in Chinese families and comes with a built-in level of respect. Calling your sibling Older Sister or Big Sister underscores that philosophy. Being the firstborn also comes with built-in responsibilities, so more is demanded of first-born children than of later siblings.

Even though my brother grew up American, is a graduate of Harvard Medical School, and practices both pediatrics and internal medicine at a prestigious hospital, he still calls me Older Sister when he calls as if we're in Taiwan in the 1960s. Then he continues the conversation in English. Over the years, I've started to call him Chi. But my parents still call him Little Brother.

The happiest times of my childhood were when my brother and sister were born. I had just turned nine and was in fourth grade when my sister was born. When my mother brought her home in a pink bundle, I was even more excited than I'd been about my brother. I would lean over her crib and gently stroke her skin and hair, calling her every cute nickname I could think of.

But now having five mouths to feed made money even tighter. We got by on my mother's low-wage factory jobs, complemented by welfare. I had vouchers for free lunch at school and eventually got a free breakfast, too. I was never ashamed of my free meals, probably because half the kids in my school got them too.

A truck from the welfare office would come by Henley Homes every other Friday to hand out free cheese, butter, flour, and other staples. To keep our qualifications current, we had to go downtown once a month and stand in a long line to get recertified. Officials had to make sure that our income was still low enough. No worries about that. My father was a graduate student who worked only during summer or as a teaching assistant with a small stipend. My mother worked at minimum-wage factory jobs.

We were given food stamps to buy groceries with, but you were restricted to what you could get. Wheaties and Total were all right, but not Cocoa Puffs. Milk and green beans, yes. Candy or potato chips, no. We also received a welfare check for our living expenses and qualified for free county health services, which administered all our vaccinations and annual checkups. Even though I was a little kid when it started, I felt fortunate and excited to be able to get those things. Those services enabled my family to get by while getting established in this country. My mother worked fifty-hour weeks, and my father practically lived at the college. We weren't freeloaders. And my brother and I grew up to be medical doctors who pay our fair share of taxes, so the help we got as a young immigrant family enabled us to eventually become contributing members of society. And that's true of most immigrant families I personally know.

We were definitely poor, but we were doing okay. And when Mingfang was diagnosed with leukemia when she was a toddler, she was able to get medical care. Her disease would be a twelve-year odyssey of hospitalizations, procedures, chemotherapy, and various other drugs. Throughout it all, she remained our Cute Little One. But all that would come later.

We stayed in Columbia, South Carolina, for several years before we packed up to follow my father to his next doctorate program. He had hit a wall in his current mathematics doctorate program after failing the verbal defense. I remember the night he came home looking as if someone had died. But I knew better than to ask. Curiosity was not encouraged in my family.

I don't know if my father ever seriously considered returning to Taiwan. He couldn't teach at a four-year university in either country without a PhD although in the United States you can teach at a two-year college with a master's degree. But after each disappointment, my father would start over. You can apply to as many PhD programs as you want, and they will admit you.

So after failing the verbal at USC, he sent out applications and had been accepted into the PhD program in computer science in the engineering department at the University of Alabama in Birmingham. And like each other time, he believed that would be the one that finally came through. It certainly seemed quixotic to me, but makes a little more sense if you understand that Taiwan is among the most highly educated countries in the world with one of the highest percentages of its citizens holding college degrees. Academic excellence was an expectation.

We made the move over the Christmas holidays, with me saying tearful good-byes to the friends I had made. Within two months we were back. It was never clear if my father had been dropped from the graduate program at the University of Alabama or if he had decided that the program wasn't right for him. Or if he left before they could kick him out. Whatever, it didn't work out. I was instructed to tell anyone who asked that the field of study didn't turn out to be what he'd signed up for.

We moved back to Columbia because we had nowhere else to go. The upside was, we'd hardly unpacked, so we just hitched a U-Haul trailer to the back of our car and stuffed all our things back into it. My father went back to the University of South Carolina and continued as a graduate student there. It was as if Alabama had been a bad, but very brief, dream.

Perhaps to clear his head or maybe just needing to remember why he had come to the United States in the first place, my father announced we were taking a family vacation. To Taiwan. To this day I have no idea how he afforded to buy the plane tickets since we always seemed to be just scraping by. I know he was always saving whatever spare money he had at the end of the week, so maybe he'd been saving since he had arrived in 1966. However he swung it, we were going to visit my parents' relatives. While the trip would connect me to my roots in an emotional way, it also cemented my identity as an American and made me profoundly appreciate my adopted country, a sentiment that still resonates today.

CULTURE SHOCK

After Chiang Kai-shek died in April 1975, his only son Chiang Ching-kuo took over leadership of Taiwan. Educated in Russia and married to a Russian national, Chiang Ching-kuo was not as authoritarian-minded as his late father, and he eased many restrictions. Although the Kuomintang party remained strong and powerful, people of Taiwan had hope things would get better.

The changes Chiang Ching-kuo enacted made Taiwanese in the United States and elsewhere less fearful about returning to visit family. So in 1976 the floodgates opened, and families that hadn't seen each other, in some cases for decades, were reunited. Or in my case, introduced.

For as long as I could remember, my parents had received aerograms from Taiwan. They never contained anything of substance. It was like one of today's emails. *We're good. Hope you're doing well. Father says hello.* In turn, my mother and father wrote similarly uninformative letters to their parents. They never sent photos either.

As much as my parents, especially my father, longed to see his relatives, there was still *thismuch* concern the KMT might detain him. So my father obtained his American citizenship before the trip. My brother and sister had been born in the United States, so they were automatically citizens. My mother and me, not so much. I guess we were considered lower risk. But that didn't mean no risk. While Taiwanese authorities didn't usually retain women or children, there was an ever-so-slight possibility that my mother and I wouldn't be allowed to fly back to the United States.

Before we left on vacation, my mother fretted constantly about the seventy-two-hour hold automatically placed on the passports of all Taiwanese citizens. When we arrived fretting had evolved into deep anxiety as my father handed over our passports so officials could check us out. The records of every Taiwanese citizen coming into the country would be checked for three days before that person's return trip abroad. If they didn't find anything on us, we would be allowed to return to the United States at the end of our visit. We could stay in Taiwan as long as we wanted, but we wouldn't find out if we could get out until three days before our planned departure. All we could do was to hope that we passed inspection.

The source for my mother's dread went back to that performance when I was six and the letter that arrived basically calling me a prepubescent trollop. Even if you didn't have a history of political activism, if any of the Kuomintang spies had reported you for bad behavior, you could be held. In order for the spies to keep getting paid, they had to earn their keep by finding some kind of dirt on somebody or just making it up. Either way. you were completely at their mercy.

My father's concerns were of an entirely different type. He had left Taiwan a decade earlier to get his PhD in the United States. He did get a master's in mathematics in 1967 at Mississippi State University, but his goal was to get a doctorate. He was embarrassed to return home without having his PhD since everyone knew that's why he had left. He decided to just say he was still working on it, which in and of itself was true, if not totally honest. But his relatives didn't know how long it was supposed to take so when he explained that you had to pass a verbal defense and a written defense, then you have to write your dissertation—which is like writing a book—and then you have to pass another written defense followed by another verbal defense, you could believe it could take more than a decade. That was his story and he was sticking to it.

力

A week before our flight I heard my parents talking in hushed, worried tones. Turns out it was about some letters my father's younger sister had written. Apparently she had missed the memo about not putting any sensitive, personal information in letters. I came to find out that over the years, she had written my father and told him that she had given birth to an illegitimate daughter who was a little younger than my brother.

This was not something the KMT would care about, but my father's family did. It was considered shameful to have a child out of wedlock. But that wasn't what the discussion was about; my father had saved all the letters and didn't know what to do with them. I guess he had stashed them away although I have no idea who he was hiding them from. But a short while later I looked out the window and saw my father standing by a garbage dumpster burning a small stack of letters. When he came back inside, he seemed relaxed and never said another word about the letters.

I was very curious about my illegitimate cousin, but I knew better than to ask even though I didn't understand why everything needed to be such a secret. The kids who were my neighbors in the projects and at school talked about their families all the time. Very little seemed off limits. Keeping secrets just seemed to cause tension and distrust. But again, I kept my opinion to myself.

Finally, the day of our flight arrived: July 4, 1976, America's bicentennial. I was both anxious and excited because I had no idea what awaited me on the other side of the world. It was a long flight. My brother found it a great adventure and was fascinated looking out the window at clouds that looked like fluffy cotton balls.

We flew from Columbia Metropolitan Airport to Los Angeles then changed planes for a flight to Guam where we had a six-hour layover. I spent most of the time trying to keep my siblings entertained until we boarded our flight to Tokyo, where we would catch a plane to Taiwan.

Walking through Tokyo airport was the first time in my conscious life to be surrounded by Asians. All my life I'd attended mostly black schools with a few whites and an occasional Chinese classmate, but for the most part I was the unique one. Here I was just another unremarkable face in the crowd. It was a surprising jolt. Being different had become the norm for me. It informed my identity. Among mostly Asian travelers you'd think I would have felt like I had come home. Instead I felt oddly out of place. I felt like a minority.

Between the flight itself and going past the International Date Line, we arrived in Taipei on July 7, three jet-lagged days after leaving South Carolina. When we got off the plane, we were greeted by a half-dozen of my father's relatives. They included my grandmother—my grandfather had died during the time my father was in the United States—and my uncle, who I would call Second Uncle.

Even though they were obviously happy to see my father and meet us, there was no hugging or tears. Everyone was very proper and reserved. Kids at my school displayed more affection and emotion on Monday mornings after not seeing their friends since Friday. Behavior I might have thought were just quirks of my particular parents turned out to be a culture-wide thing.

My father's relatives had driven more than two hundred miles from their hometown on the southern coast of Taiwan to get us all the way north to Taipei to await our arrival. Second Uncle and my grandmother had reserved two rooms for that night in a nearby hotel: one room for my family and one for the other relatives. I appreciated my grandmother's organization; my father had clearly not inherited that gene. During our quick ride to the hotel, my grandmother and father were engrossed in conversation, trying to catch up on one another's lives. My mother was very quiet. I was just ten, but I was aware enough to get the impression she and her mother-in-law didn't get along that well.

Even though my father's relatives had met us at the airport, we made our way to spend time with my mother's family in Tainan first. Then we went to my father's hometown, Nahpee. Then we traveled back and forth between Tainan and Nahpee several more times during our stay, apparently to give both sides of the family equal time and attention. I'm not sure what family politics were playing out between my parents and their respective families that determined who we visited when, but it entailed an awful lot of travel. The trip between Tainan and the village of Nahpee took half a day each way because of all the stops. When my father was enlisted to go talk to his younger sister about her single mom status, my mother and us kids stayed in Tainan while my father traveled alone back to Nahpee.

The two different sides of the family were a study in contrasts. Just like my parents themselves. While my parents reconnected with their families and cultural roots, it gave me context for why my parents were the way they were. It didn't necessarily eliminate my wistfulness or resentment. It would have been nice if my father would simply find a decent-paying job teaching high school math in Columbia or somewhere so his children could enjoy a middle-class life with permanent roots rather than drag them from one welfare apartment to the next pursuing one PhD program after another. What others might have seen as dedication, I saw as selfishness.

Obviously, the finer points of understanding my parents came later as an adult with a career and family of my own. But even as a ten-year-old, I saw my parents in a new light after that trip although not necessarily in a better light.

力

On the way to Tainan by train, we made a detour to Taichung to visit my adopted great-aunt. My father's brother and mother were traveling with us, and we all spent the night. My paternal grandfather had one brother and no sisters. Back then if you had children of only one gender, you would informally adopt a child of the other gender from some nearby relative who had several children of each and then raise that child as your own. So my grandparents had adopted my great aunt. She was very gracious and generous, preparing food as if we hadn't eaten since leaving the United States.

The next day we left my father's family behind and caught a train for Tainan City, where both my mother and I had been born. The trip took forever because the train stopped at every city along the way. My mother had not seen her parents since 1968. They were in their eighties by the time of our visit but still very healthy, regularly climbing six flights of stairs to a rooftop terrace, where my grandfather tended an impressive bonsai garden. My maternal grandparents and all of my mother's relatives treated us wonderfully. I met my mother's only brother—Uncle on the Mother's Side. We went to parks and drank gallons of Orange Fanta, which was apparently the Taiwanese soda of choice.

My maternal grandparents' house, where I had lived after my father had left for America, was very nice but missing amenities I took for granted having grown up in the United States. Like flush toilets and sewer systems. They didn't have refrigeration, either. Food was stored in a cupboard. Anything perishable had to be eaten within a day of bringing it home from the market.

Both my grandmothers kept spotless homes. I attribute this to the Japanese education they received when Taiwan was under Japanese occupation. My parents' generation, growing up during the regime of Chiang Kai-shek, was nowhere near as neat and tidy. Both grandmothers' hair was always combed perfectly in place, and their homes were organized with almost military precision. If my parents had made enough money to buy things, they'd have been hoarders by comparison.

Even without modern amenities, it was clear my parents had grown up in more stable surroundings than my siblings and I were accustomed to. My mother's family, the Wangs, were decidedly middle class, which in Taiwan is almost considered privileged, and they lived in Tainan, a cosmopolitan city that also happens to be Taiwan's oldest city. Her family was financially secure, so she never had to worry about having enough money to pay the bills.

My little brother and I loved our maternal grandparents' six-story house because it was a great place to explore. It was built like a narrow stack of blocks, with only two rooms on each level, connected by steep flights of stairs. The first floor was rented out as a storefront. My grandparents occupied the rest of the floors.

My grandparents slept in separate rooms, following an Asian custom that it's not proper to be seen in the same bed together even if married. Any intimacy occurred after the rest of the family had gone to sleep, then it was back to their respective rooms once the encounter ended. Not terribly romantic.

But it was a hard house to sleep in because there was no air conditioning and in July, Taiwan was hot and humid. You had no choice but to sleep with the windows open, which was an open invitation to an assortment of lizards, mosquitoes, and other critters.

My father's village was a world apart. My father's fishing village was called Lin Pien in Mandarin and Nahpee in Taiwanese. Nahpee is in Taiwan's poorest county in Taiwan, even though it boasts the most fertile farmland in the entire country and abundant fishing. By Asian tradition my father's birthplace is considered his children's hometown regardless of where we were physically born. And interestingly, I connected with my Taiwanese roots in Nahpee more than I did in Tainan.

The first person I met in Nahpee was my great-grand-mother at her home, the place where my father had grown up. She was blind and hunched over from age, but happy, clean, and well cared for. You could still see the bond between her and my father. Apparently, my great-grand-mother's home had not changed since the 1930s. There was a yard in the middle surrounded by rooms with low ceilings and no doors. Chickens roamed about, and water came from a manual pump. It was definitely rustic.

My father's parents lived in a modest two-story house. They weren't as well off as my mother's parents, but by Nahpee's standards they were middle-class and lived a comfortable life. My father's relatives celebrated his visit by setting off firecrackers. Apparently, my father was well-known in Nahpee for having gone to America. Nobody else in my father's family had ever left their little coastal fishing community. During the entire decade he'd been gone, only two other villagers had left Nahpee for other parts of Taiwan or beyond. By and large people born in the village lived and died in the village. For someone who had lived in six different cities and towns by the age of ten, it was hard to imagine.

While in Nahpee my family and my grandmother crammed into a friend's car to go visit my grandfather's grave. I was expecting him to be in a cemetery like we have in the United States. But he wasn't. My grandfather's grave was in the open countryside. There were no gate or road signs to indicate that people were buried there. I later learned that in Taiwan you rented the ground where your family member was buried from the local landowner. So this hillside where my grandfather was interred was not a designated cemetery but private land that could be sold at any time to someone else.

We climbed up a hill covered in long grass, and then right in the middle of nowhere were four crypts poking out of the ground. They looked like little houses made of brick or stone, and one of them was my grandfather's. The custom is to burn incense by the grave, so the smoke will summon the spirits of the dead person's ancestors to accompany them on their afterlife journey. After lighting the incense we bowed and recited a rite, observed a few minutes of silence, then walked down the hill and piled back into the car. I imagined the spirit of my grandfather watching us drive away.

Back in Tainan I saw another ritual for the dead: a Taiwanese funeral. The thing that first stands out is that everyone wears white, which is the color associated with mourning—and purity—by Chinese culture. I had first encountered this difference when I was scolded by someone at either a Chinese New Year or Autumn Festival event. Apparently the white shirt I was wearing under my jumper was inappropriate. Why my mother had ignored that cultural no-no I'm not sure although in the scheme of faux pas it seems a low priority.

Growing up in America, I had never attended a funeral, but I'd seen processions of cars with their lights on following a hearse. And South Carolina, which was one of the original thirteen colonies, had many old cemeteries. Some graves were modest, some had impressive headstones, some were well-tended with flowers.

When going with my father to the university in the summer, we'd pass by some mortuaries and funeral homes. They always looked kind of creepy, all somber and gray.

There never seemed to be anyone entering or leaving. Other than the occasional car procession, funerals seemed to be very private affairs that took place out of sight. So it was a surprise when we were at my mother's family home in Tainan—which faced one of the city's main commercial streets—and one morning we heard the sound of cymbals clanging. There was another sound too, like a very shrill, metallic clarinet. I later learned the instrument making that sound was a Chinese suona, which is a double-reed woodwind made of wood and copper. If Mariah Carey hitting the high notes was reincarnated as a musical instrument, it would be a suona.

Curious, I ran to a window and saw a group of people marching down the street in between the bicycles, motorcycles, mopeds, and a few cars, creating a bit of a traffic logjam. Fifteen or so mourners dressed in colorful red costumes but wearing somber expressions formed a small parade, accompanied by the cymbals' and suonas' dirge, that continued past the house and up the street. Nobody on the street seemed concerned or surprised as they moved out of the way to let the parade pass. No one stopped to gawk. I seemed to be the only one.

"What kind of parade is going on?" I asked my mother.

"That's a funeral procession for someone who died."

After a few minutes they disappeared around a corner although I could still hear their instruments on the air. I was really confused. This was so different from what I had previously learned about traditional Taiwanese funerals. I had thought that when someone died, you didn't wear anything red or black; you wore white all over. White represents death, which is why it's proper to wear all white to Taiwanese funerals. So I didn't understand why those people were wearing festive red.

I asked my relatives, and they explained how the parade represented the soul's last walk through the city, the dead person's last spiritual hurrah. So participants were celebrating the deceased's life through the costumes and music. In New Orleans they do a similar celebration called a jazz funeral with a procession through the streets accompanied by a jazz band. Seems a lot of cultures pave the way to eternity through music.

力

The three weeks passed quickly, and soon enough we were packing to go home. Our relatives were aware that this family trip had been a special occurrence unlikely to happen again any time soon. If ever. So when they said good-bye, they meant good-bye. Both grandmothers gave me photos to keep and the memories made would literally last a lifetime.

We'd been so busy that I hadn't thought much about whether or not my mother and I would be allowed to leave Taiwan. But those fears bubbled back to the surface during the train ride back to Taipei, and I prepared for the worst as we entered the airport. All that anxiety was anticlimactic. The officials stamped our passports, and we boarded the plane. This time our flight went to Hawaii, where we went through Customs and Immigration. Then we boarded another flight that would take us back home to South Carolina.

And it did feel like going home. On one side of me, my father fell asleep watching a movie with my little brother on his lap. On my other side, my mother and baby sister slept soundly. I took out the handful of snapshots my grandparents had given me. I had grown to love these people, and as it turned out, I would never see most of them ever again.

Once back in Columbia, I felt more American than ever. Home was sweet compared to Taiwan. I had never worried before about my father moving back to Taiwan, but now I thought about it a lot. I was worried that my parents might consider Taiwan as a Plan B if my father continued falling out of these PhD programs. I could feel them entertaining that possibility, and it was incomprehensible to me.

In America there's a sense of freedom that doesn't exist in Taiwan. It's ingrained in the country's DNA. Even in the most partisan of times, the United States more than any other country is open to ideas. If you don't like one city, you have the freedom to move to another. If you work hard enough, you can be anything you want regardless of what political party you do or don't belong to. You can express your beliefs. You can publish your book. Even the busiest cities are not cramped the way Taiwan is.

That three-week trip also gave me a profound appreciation for modern plumbing, kitchen appliances, and window-mounted air conditioners. The poorest American home in 1976 was rich compared to a typical middle-class home in Taiwan when it came to modern amenities that we view here as necessities, not luxuries, for our health and wellness.

So I made my own plan. I resolved to work harder and excel in school, go to college, become an MD, and stay in the United States. Permanently. I wanted to succeed where my father hadn't. As I prepared for a new school year in August 1976, I couldn't wait to start middle school and study like crazy to get ahead.

Over the following years, I became increasingly

curious if my attitudes about my family, our culture, and my personal ambitions were unique to me and my situation or if it was common among other Taiwanese immigrant children. I would have the opportunity to find out as my father became closer to three Taiwanese families who each happened to have a daughter around my age. I would end up having lifelong contact with these young women and find we did have a lot in common although we ended up taking very different paths in life.

5

PAT

Because both my parents worked, for most of my elementary school years I had pre- and after-school babysitters. They were usually neighbors who already had kids going to my school so what was one more. It was through these families that I first saw American family dynamics in action. The kids were boisterous and weren't afraid to express themselves. One set of siblings took swearing to an art form and did their best to spice up my vocabulary with some choice blue words. A family that babysat me for a long while introduced me to American television and family dinners full of conversation and teasing. The parents were occasionally exasperated, so there was lots of yelling but also lots of hugs. The apartments were messy and lived-in but also welcoming. And while the dad may have brought home the bacon, the mamas definitely ruled the roost.

It was like an alt-universe compared to my family and other Taiwanese families I knew. My mother in particular would have been horrified at the lack of decorum. But to me it was a shot of oxygen, both fun and exhilarating while also bittersweet. While I preferred tidiness—none of my babysitters were ace housekeepers—I could still see what childhood looked like for other kids my age. And it wasn't what mine looked like. Because my mother couldn't speak English and my father was too preoccupied with his studies, I ended up being the family personal secretary. I had to pay bills, respond to any letters from creditors or school, make the doctor's appointments, and organize our babysitting. As the eldest daughter, it was expected of me.

While some of our household structure was based on Taiwanese culture—stay quiet, never talk back, do not express a contrary opinion, excel at school—some was simply a product of my particular parents. And as I got older and spent time around some of our Taiwanese family friends, it became easier to see which was which.

As everybody, especially kids, know, like Dante's circles of hell, there are different levels of friends, from BFF to frenemies and all the permutations in between. The children of my babysitters were friends of circumstance. Once I switched babysitters, I had little to no contact with them anymore. Classmate friends came and went with each grade. My best friend was Janine, a black girl who helped me channel my inner African-American, tried to teach me to dance, and helped me develop a sense of independence. Tall and solid, she was my protector and made sure nobody messed with me. I was heartbroken when we had to leave Columbia so my father could start yet another PhD program, this one in Texas. When we reconnected forty years later when I attended her second wedding, that bond remained.

The daughters of my father's Taiwanese friends were family friends. I met them at a young age, and for a period of time, they each became a constant in my life. Over the years I kept in touch, almost the way you do with some relatives, sharing updates. The same thing Twitter and Facebook do now in real time. While we were not confidantes, we belonged to the same sorority, growing up in one culture while raised by another. Our immigrant parents were certainly freer, but whether or not they were completely happy wasn't always obvious. At least when visiting these other families, they had a sense of the home they had left.

力

When we were in Rock Hill during my father's tenure at Friendship College, there wasn't much socializing. We were stuck on campus, and it was a very insular kind of existence. But once we got to Columbia, my parents became slightly more social, in an insular kind of way. My father became acquainted with Dr. Woo, who had earned his PhD in mathematics at Notre Dame and was now teaching math at South Carolina State College in Orangeburg, which was forty miles from Rock Hill. Despite his top-tier credentials, Dr. Woo did not speak English very well, so he had a hard time finding work at a major university, which is why he ended up at an all-black state college.

Starting when I was about five, one Friday a month we would make the hour drive to Orangeburg so Dr. Woo could help my dad by checking his math proofs, and then they would visit and talk for hours. We'd arrive around seven or eight o'clock, and they would huddle together in the kitchen often until midnight.

My mother and Mrs. Woo would sit in the living room together, chatting to pass the time, and I would hang out with their daughter, Pat. I was older by a couple of years, but we were the same size. We'd go into her room and play with her toys and dolls. At home my spare time was filled with doing math problems my parents gave me, so I enjoyed going to the Woos' because Pat had a lot of toys. They also lived in faculty housing but had much nicer things because Dr. Woo was a full professor and teaching full time. They had a piano, and Pat had a little table with a little phone. And they had Jell-O. I don't know that I was jealous of Pat. But I was aware her standard of living was a lot better than mine.

For as long as we lived in Columbia, we'd have a monthly visit with the Woos. Sometimes my mother would bring some dried noodles, and Mrs. Woo would cook them so we could have dinner together. That one evening was the extent of their socializing or contact. We didn't have a phone, so it wasn't like they could talk in between visits.

One topic my father and Dr. Woo always discussed was Taiwanese politics. Dr. Woo was very anti-Chiang Kai-shek, as was my father. But Dr. Woo was much more of an activist than my parents. He helped organize many of the anti-Kuomintang groups in South Carolina and other southern states. Dr. Woo had left Taiwan for the same reason that my father did. He didn't want to join the Kuomintang and pledge fealty to their ideology. Dr. Woo also was against martial law and deeply resented not being legally allowed to speak Taiwanese at home or anywhere else.

After we started visiting his family regularly, Dr. Woo introduced us to other Taiwanese families in the area. One lived just down the street from us, an English professor who was teaching at a black college. We also met the Chen family in Greenville. The father had earned his PhD in mathematics or statistics and was doing actuarial work at Liberty Mutual. We spent one Christmas with these two families, everybody happily speaking Taiwanese.

Eventually both my family and the Woos left South Carolina. In our case it was because my father got accepted to yet another PhD program in Texas. Pat moved after her father got a very stable job at a good company in New Jersey. We stayed in touch by writing letters—this was long before the advent of email. Although we wrote each other religiously—almost always two-page, handwritten letters in English—we really didn't know that much about who the other really was. We recounted events but not how we felt about things. I found it interesting that her personality in the letters was much warmer than her aloofness in person, but she became increasingly distant as she got older.

The Woos settled in New Jersey, and Pat enjoyed a stable home life through her teens and into college. Living the transient lifestyle we did because of my father's academic shortfalls, I was more wistful than envious. I obviously ended up okay, but it would have been nice to go through childhood not having to constantly worry about being uprooted. Or homeless.

Years later, Mrs. Woo commented that I had endured a rough childhood, but she was glad that my adulthood was happy and secure.

"For my daughter, it was the opposite," she observed. "Her childhood and adolescence were wonderful. Her adult life was not."

Pat and I continued our letter writing all through college. She was accepted by Boston University's six-year MD program, which combined two years of college and four years of medical school into six years, with all requirements satisfied. It was a very accelerated program for the very few and very smart. Acceptance does not guarantee graduation; they weed out students every year. Pat made it all the way to the end.

I guess it was inevitable we both married Taiwanese men. My husband had grown up in Taiwan while Pat's was born in the United States in 1967, not long after his parents had immigrated. While my suffocating home life led me to accept Doc's marriage proposal on our first date, Pat waited until later in life.

In the 1980s most people got married before their thirties, especially children of Taiwanese immigrants. Pat's parents were getting ever more anxious with each passing year their daughter stayed single. But at the same time, they wanted approval over who she married. They were adamant she marry another Taiwanese. They disapproved if she dated anyone white, anyone Jewish, even one guy because he was going bald.

When Pat hit thirty, the desperate elder Woos took action. Pat's father knew the president and founder of one of the subversive anti-KMT groups; her parents had known the man and his wife since the 1970s. That couple had a son who was also single. So the parents played matchmaker. To them it was perfect: the son was Taiwanese (actually, he was American since he was born in the United States, but that was just a technicality to the Woos), and his parents were ardently anti-KMT. They would have never accepted a nationalist.

It's hard to say if Pat and the other family's son would have hit it off as a couple if they had met on their own. But as it was their marriage was not about romance. It was about expedience, at least in the beginning. It was the next best thing to an arranged marriage. Despite having gone away to college and becoming a physician, she was still submissive enough to let her parents have a significant say in who she married. More irony: the Woos ended up disliking their son-in-law, feeling Pat had married down.

In 2007 when she was thirty-eight, Pat was diagnosed with advanced colon cancer: stage four adenocarcinoma. After weeks of constipation, Pat went to the ER doubled over in pain. Surgeons discovered a 95 percent occlusion caused by a huge mass in her anal-rectal area. They removed half her intestines, but they also discovered it had spread to her lymph nodes.

When I learned of her diagnosis, I flew to Virginia the following month and reconnected with her. We had not seen each other for nearly twenty years. Since we were both physicians, we spent countless conversations going over her diagnosis and options, including new, cutting-edge treatments. We also tried to figure out the unknowable: why? Had she inherited a cancer gene? Had stress compromised her immune system? Were environmental toxins the culprit? Human beings always want a reason; they want to have something they can blame. Random chance just doesn't sit well with us as a species. Makes us feel too vulnerable.

During that visit we talked honestly about our upbringing for the first time. Pat was surprised at how controlling my mother had been, which explained in part why I got married at nineteen. She couldn't fathom that I had never been allowed to go to a high school football game, dance, or function. How my mother insisted I live at home when I enrolled in college.

"I thought my mother was bad," Pat said. "Your mother was oppressive. At least my mother let me go away to college and live in a dorm and have a normal life. I can't believe your mother didn't."

The irony, of course, being that they had fled their homeland because of oppression and yet my mother restricted my independence, interactions, and freedom of choice just as tightly.

After Pat's operation in 2007, she recovered and appeared to be in remission. The following year I flew out for another visit, which was quite different from the first. Pat had not been outgoing as a kid, and it had taken her a while to warm up to me. Honestly, I discovered I liked her a lot better once we stopped seeing each other in person and began writing because she came across much more friendly in her letters than she had ever been in face-to-face conversation.

Her cancer diagnosis and uncertain future had seemed to bring down some of those walls on the last trip out. But on my second visit she was back to her standoffish self. And then some. It's Taiwanese tradition for a guest to help in the kitchen before a meal and help clean up afterward. So on the first evening of my second visit, I was standing next to Pat at the sink husking corn. When I tossed the husks and corn silk into the garbage pail under the sink, she shouted at me, her voice shrill.

"Don't do that! That's for the *compost*." She wasn't just annoyed; she sounded angry.

Okay, that took me aback. I had just spent $1000 for my round-trip flight to Virginia from Texas, and I was just helping keep the kitchen neat. Her reaction seemed out of proportion. And in my defense, I'd never heard of anyone who had a home composting setup, but I apologized profusely. When someone is ill or has been through some serious challenges, you make exceptions and let things go.

Still, it got me thinking. I wondered if her distance and edginess were because she had grown uncomfortable that I knew so much about her condition. In Taiwanese culture illness was considered a very private thing. Not so much out of concern for the patient but because of how it might reflect on the family.

When she was two and a half, my sister was diagnosed with acute lymphocytic leukemia. Her doctors told my parents that Mingfang couldn't be cured; they could only prolong her life. From that moment on, my parents kept her cancer hidden from even their closest friends like the Woos because they were afraid outsiders—especially other Taiwanese—would think that our family had bad genes, which would hurt my brother's and my marriage prospects. Who'd want us if we might be carrying cancer? But it went beyond that because we never even discussed it as a family. It was the elephant in the room. And still is. To this day my parents have never discussed her illness and the heartbreak of losing her.

Even when I first heard about Pat's diagnosis, I was surprised at how advanced it was because she should have been experiencing noticeable symptoms for a while. And she was a physician, so she should have been especially aware something was wrong. It made me sad to think she might have ignored the symptoms because of some misguided, ingrained cultural taboo. Then again some people ignore symptoms out of fear.

Pat fought her cancer for seven years, undergoing chemo and other treatments. It bought her time but not a cure. By the end of 2013, the cancer had metastasized. At forty-five she was living on borrowed time. Over her final year, the disease ravaged her body. She went into hospice in October 2014. At the end she suffered from severe swelling of her legs, difficulty breathing, and had lost her vision. But her mind remained clear.

Starting from Thanksgiving her doctors told the family she was day-to-day, and they started saying good-bye. I was getting regular updates from her husband. They put the phone to her ear so I could talk to her. It was heartbreaking. Both Pat's sister and husband promised to let me know when she passed. That call came on December 13. She left behind two children.

A few years later I called Dr. Woo after sending him a copy of one of my books. When I was growing up, he went by his Taiwanese name, Hsi-Shi. But now he went by Warren. That seemed rather random.

"So where does this name Warren come from?" I asked.

He explained that when he relocated to his job in New Jersey, he found it easier to use an American name and it helped him assimilate. *Yeah, but why Warren?* Apparently that was the name that one of his colleagues called him. Really random.

We stayed on the phone for over an hour, talking about how I was doing, how my parents were doing—just catching up. Afterward, he sent me an email.

> Dear Chiufang,
>
> Thank you very much for sending me your memoir. Certainly I will be enjoying reading your memoir that will fill up my memory about your grown-up childhood, which is pretty much incomplete in my memory.
>
> We are very happy to be able to eye-witness you from a very small girl to now being well-established with a successful medical career.

Everyone in this world has one's own life journey which may not be always smooth and happy. So we would be satisfied with whatever we have now, hope for better tomorrow, and not be burdened by past sorrows.

We regret that we did not have much time to get together before. We hope we should make an effort to take our time to see each other in the future. Let us all take good care of ourselves for our future getting together.

God be with you all.

Love,

Warren and Irene Woo

Even though Pat is gone, I've kept up my friendship with her husband and her parents, who I regularly have long phone calls with. Her mother still complains about her son-in-law. I always think: *Be careful what you wish for.* Staying in touch with Pat's relatives keeps her alive for me. And our ongoing relationship helps us all manage our respective loss.

Our wedding day. We were happy but our parents ... not so much. But it still ended up being a great day and definitely exceeded my expectations.

白色恐怖政治受難者紀念碑

IN MEMORY OF THE VICTIMS OF THE WHITE TERROR

A memorial to honor the victims of the White Terror, located in 228 Peace Park.

Baby William with his parents.

Three generations. My parents, Doc and I, and our two sons, Barrington and Abraham.

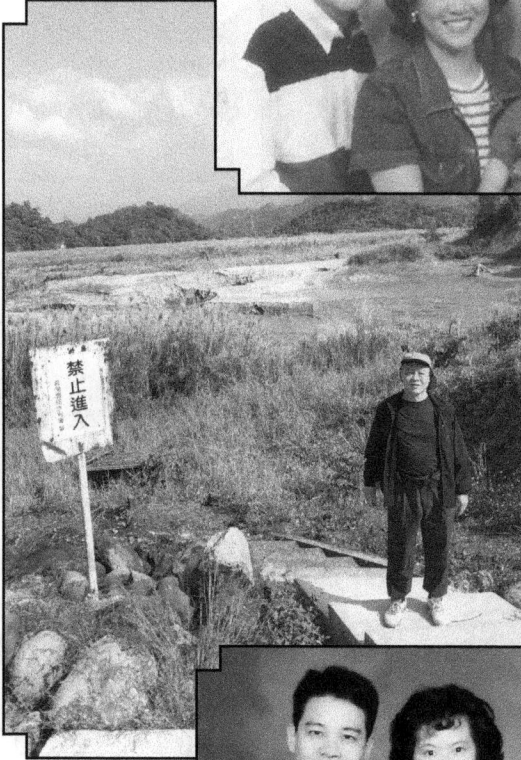

Doc visiting Tainan's Baihe District where he grew up. Today the area is known for its hot springs and Lotus Festival.

Doc and I, his parents and sister, and two-year-old Barrington.

Mary and I out at dinner. A brainiac, she attended both Harvard and Yale on her way to becoming a doctor.

Taipei's night markets are famous for their food, which is fresh and usually cooked to order. It's like an endless buffet.

With my brother.

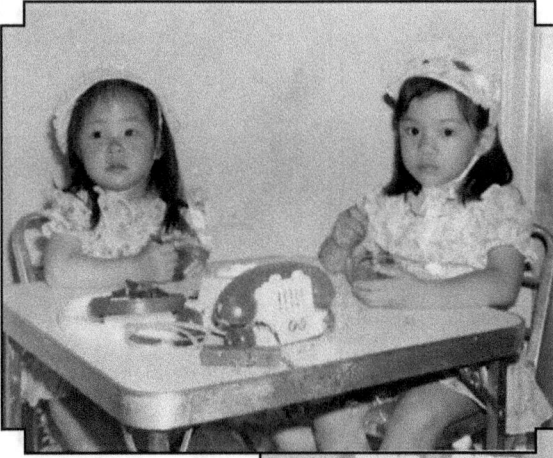

Pat and I having a snack. Why we look like we're wearing Easter bonnets, I have no idea. But neither of us look particularly thrilled about it.

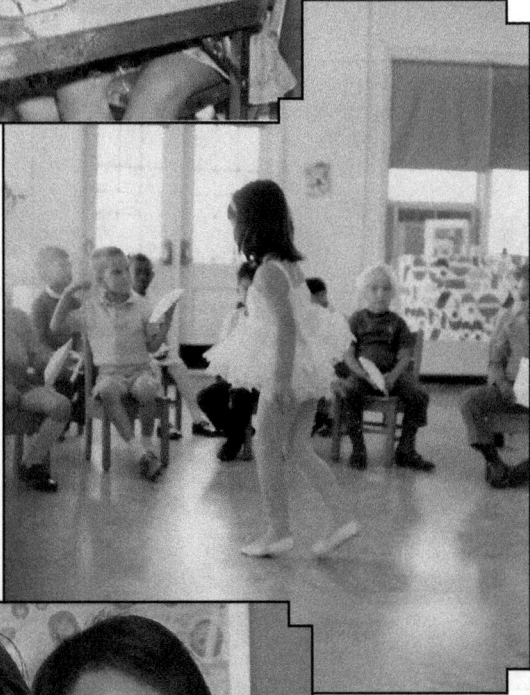

Showing off my moves at Henley Homes kindergarten graduation.

Pat and me forty years later, much happier.

Taiwan is known for its temples but none are as famous as Longshan Temple, which was built in 1738.

Doc and I at Barrington's white coat ceremony.

With my friend Annie. A lawyer by training, Annie teaches full time at a university in Washington, DC.

6

ANNIE

After my mother and I arrived in the United States, we lived a transient life for the next nine years, hop-scotching around the South, uprooted every time my father left one PhD program for another. We stayed the longest in Columbia, where I made my closest American friend, Janine. But inevitably we moved again when I was twelve.

My parents never knew it, but for about a year I spent a couple hours every weekday afternoon riding the city bus around Columbia just to see what I could see. Not all of it was pretty; Columbia had some mean streets. But it was more interesting than being a latchkey kid. My parents had stopped paying to have after-school babysitting for me, believing I was old enough to be home alone for a couple of hours. I figured if I was old enough for that, I was old enough to go on my bus excursions. Janine insisted on coming along to make sure nothing happened to me. We became inseparable.

Then I found out we were moving to College Station

where my father had been accepted at Texas A&M's computer science doctorate program. I don't know if it was denial or not wanting our last days together to be filled with sadness, but I waited until my last day in Columbia before telling her we were leaving. Of course, I told her when we were on the bus. We both cried. A lot. I didn't get emotional at the thought of leaving Pat and the Woos, but I felt a loss leaving Janine, my friend and protector who I dearly loved. It would be forty years before we saw each other again.

When our family got to College Station, my father looked up an old friend, Mr. Chen. They had become acquainted not long after my mother and I joined him in the United States in 1968. Like my father, Mr. Chen had emigrated from Taiwan and had been in a doctorate program at the University of Texas at Austin. When he didn't succeed, he took a job as an instructor at Prairie View A&M University, where he met my father, who was also new to the school. They were both fervently anti-Kuomintang and got to know each other. The Chens had a son who was a year younger than me. We were the only Taiwanese families there, which was the primary basis of the friendship.

The Chens now lived in Houston, which was about an hour and a half away from College Station, and my father rekindled their friendship. So we started visiting them regularly, driving out once or twice a month on a Saturday. Mr. Chen had become quite successful since my father had last seen him. After his time at Prairie View, Mr. Chen got a very good job at Texas Instruments in Houston, enabling the family to enjoy a very comfortable suburban lifestyle in Sugar Land. In their neighborhood all the houses were brick, with green lawns out front and private backyard separated by wooden fences. Each house had a two-car garage.

When I first met Annie I was twelve, and she was five years old. Because her brother and I were closer in age, at first I interacted more with him than with Annie, even though he was a quiet boy. Like my family, the elder Chens were socially isolated. Mrs. Chen seemed withdrawn to the point of depressed. But unlike my mother she didn't work, so she was stuck at home all day. As time went on we children became very close. I really liked interacting with Annie and her brother.

A typical visit would have us leave home late Saturday morning, get to the Chens' home around noon. We would park in the driveway and walk to the back of the house and enter through the kitchen. We never came empty-handed; my mother would bring dried noodles or some other dish. My parents would plop themselves down at the kitchen table and remain there for hours. When four Taiwanese adults get together, there is a lot of talk and not much action. We'd eat lunch and then our parents—mostly our fathers—chatted all day about politics in Taiwan and whatever else while us kids would go off and hang out in their spacious house—which had blessed central air conditioning—then we'd eat dinner there too.

As with the Woos, my parents never reciprocated by inviting the Chens over to our one-bedroom apartment. It would have been a very tight squeeze—my siblings and I slept on folding cots in the living room, so there wasn't a lot of spare space. And during the summer, it would be unbearably hot having nine people in our apartment.

But the Chens didn't mind being the designated hosts. They welcomed us because they and my parents shared the same native language and background. They were at ease with each other. And I was at ease with Annie and her brother. I also enjoyed the luxury of their house with its tiled floors and carpeted rooms. Master bedrooms even had their own bathrooms, which I had never seen before. They had a large kitchen, and their garage was filled with tools, all neatly hung on pegboards. It felt palatial.

Mr. Chen was a bit of an anomaly. He'd ultimately stay at TI for about twenty years, going from engineer to managerial positions. But most of the Taiwanese men my father's age that I had met embodied a PhD-or-bust mentality. For some reason taking a secure job such as teaching high school and living a modest but comfortable life with a regular paycheck wasn't an option. Those who failed to get their doctoral degrees acted like if they couldn't teach college, they shouldn't teach at all. Instead they often ended up becoming small business owners of true mom-and-pop joints.

For example, once when my family went to an anti-KMT summer camp, this one near Austin in the late 1970s, I was very excited because we were going to stay at a motel, which to me would be a special treat. We pulled up to a place that made the Bates Motel in *Psycho* look inviting. It was dilapidated with weather-worn paint and apparently was a favorite of the local hookers because you could literally rent a room by the hour. The neon *No Vacancy* sign was half on, half off, so it wasn't clear if there were any vacancies or not—until you saw the place. My guess is there were always vacancies. We got our key and drove right up to the room, which didn't look too secure.

It was owned by a Taiwanese man who had earned a master's degree but never achieved his PhD. Because of that he felt he couldn't go back to Taiwan and hope to get any decent job. In the 1970s it was hard to go back to Taiwan if you had failed because Chiang Kai-shek was still very much in control, and it would mean admitting to your family in person you had failed. So this man had bought a motel. And now it was his livelihood. I guess I should be grateful my father kept trying to get his doctorate or who knows where we might have ended up.

In case you're wondering if my father finally earned his doctorate at Texas A&M, the answer is no. Midwestern State University in Wichita Falls, Texas, tentatively offered him a position for the following academic year, with renewal contingent on receipt of his PhD. The plan was that he would teach in Wichita Falls and come back to College Station once a month to meet with his advisor and complete his dissertation. But ultimately his dissertation was not accepted, which meant his teaching contract at MSU would not be renewed. So after a year in Wichita Falls we returned to College Station.

The irony in all this was that I'm not sure my father particularly enjoyed mathematics, so maybe he just wasn't cut out to be a mathematician. In Taiwan back in the 1960s everyone had to take an entrance exam for college. If you passed, your score determined which college or university you'd attend as well as what you were to study. A student couldn't choose their major. The state chose for you. The very top scorers were placed in a medical school program. My father's exam score determined that he would be a math major. Apparently it never occurred to him to switch majors to something he liked better. But his undergraduate degrees were in math, so he doggedly stayed on that path. Until he didn't.

In the summer of 1983, he took a three-month programming job in San Jose, California, and while there found out about Kensington University in Santa Monica. It was a university in title only. In reality it was an unaccredited college, a nice way of saying a diploma-mill, which the state of California would eventually shut down in 2003.

My father did not attend classes there; neither did anyone else. Instead he submitted proof of the PhD coursework he had completed at Texas A&M. Kensington approved the coursework, and then they evaluated his dissertation, sending it back and forth a few times for some cursory revisions. The charade continued for a year, and in return for a diploma of dubious merit, my father paid Kensington's high fees. After it was closed I read where they charged as much as $20,000. But when Kensington approved his dissertation, its provenance be damned.

Afterward, when people asked if he had a PhD, he would say yes. He even puts the Dr. title in front of his name. His family assumed his degree was from Texas A&M because he said he had done his PhD work there, which is true. But he doesn't claim that he graduated from there because he never did. That degree from an unaccredited facility did not gain him entree into a university professorship. But it boosted his self-esteem. And in July 1990 it led to a job as a professor of mathematics and computer science at Houston Community Southeast College, where he would stay the rest of his career. Mind you, he could have gotten the same job with his master's; you don't need a PhD to teach at a community college so really, we lived a Bedouin lifestyle for his ego.

Even as a child I was aware how different my father was from Mr. Chen. He was organized, on top of things, didn't procrastinate. His lawn was always meticulously mowed, not a weed or overgrown blade of grass visible. He was no doubt a little OCD, which is probably what made him such a good employee.

Materially their house was very nice, but there was turmoil at home; it was a classic case of things not being what they seemed from the outside. I remember on one of our visits I noticed there was a gaping hole near the bottom of the door to Mr. and Mrs. Chen's bedroom. A month earlier when we had visited the door had been intact.

Granted it was a hollow core door so even as a diminutive young teen I could have probably kicked a hole in it myself. But it wasn't the physical damage that was shocking; it was the underlying emotion that had caused the destruction that was unnerving. Someone had tried stuffing the hole with paper or cloth. The poor attempt to cover up the hole somehow made it worse.

I got Annie's attention, motioned to the door, and raised my eyebrows. "Your dad?" I whispered.

Annie, who was about six then, said quietly, "Yeah," then looked at the floor.

Years later Annie and I talked about what she had experienced growing up, specifically the subject of her father's violent behavior. Even if Annie hadn't been forthcoming about it, I had been aware even as a kid that something was amiss. There were plenty of signs such as things that had been thrown and broken.

When I visited Annie in 2015, she admitted how volatile he was. Her parents' marriage had long been rocky, and even back when we were kids, they weren't getting along. But they would put up a good front, pretending everything was fine when we visited or when they were out in public. But I remembered how as a kid I sensed their smiles were superficial and noticed how they never really engaged with one another. But it was not something as a kid that I would ever ask about.

But as an adult—a long-married adult—I knew my

childhood suspicions had been quite accurate. So, during a visit I made to Annie in 2015, we talked about her parents and what it was like growing up in that atmosphere. It would have never occurred to us to share such confidences as children. American teens confide everything to their friends, in part because telling your troubles to a close friend is comforting and also empowering because it means you are not in denial over what is going on. But in the Asian culture, revealing family troubles to outsiders is taboo, doubly so for those who endure domestic violence. Annie had never discussed it, not even with her brother.

I thought it interesting that Annie put the blame squarely on her father, believing her mother was blameless for the acrimony. I thought back to my impressions of Mrs. Chen, and they were unremarkable: withdrawn, solitary, passive, and often asleep. I could see why Annie's father was so volatile. When a man is that driven to be successful—coming to the United States requires a certain amount of ambition—then doesn't get the doctorate that drove them, it emotionally wears on them. I am in no way saying it is right, but many men will channel that disappointment and embarrassment into aggression. No matter how good of a job he got, failing to get his PhD remained a festering frustration. Obviously, success at your job can mitigate the frustration but it never completely eliminates it.

A fulfilling relationship can also take the edge off life's disappointments. But Mrs. Chen seemed miserable. She wasn't active or joyful and seemed to prefer staying home inside her own little shell. She had come from a wealthy, successful family who might have looked down on Mr. Chen for not getting his PhD, causing her to lose face. That became bitterness and resentment toward her husband. That is very common in Taiwan culture.

Also, Mrs. Chen came from a super-wealthy family who ran a paper mill. Back in the 1940s and 1950s, paper was a hot ticket, almost as valuable as oil fields. So Annie's mother was an actual paper heiress. Mr. Chen came from a family of modest means. Mrs. Chen had access to a lot of family money—more money than Mr. Chen could probably ever earn. Financial inequality remains an issue between men and women in many cultures; it's not just an Asian thing. Men generally want to feel that they are the breadwinners, the ones taking care of the family. If the wife or significant other make them feel like they failed because they can't match her wealth, it can cause resentments that boil over. That's poison for any marriage.

My mother's family was very comfortable financially, but they weren't rich. They couldn't afford to buy us a house in the United States and support us. So my parents didn't have that tension. But my mother did have resentments, mostly because of our peripatetic lifestyle. My father seemed oblivious to putting down roots, but the rest of us would have liked that kind of security.

I never saw Mr. Chen mistreat Annie, but he was harsh and cold toward her brother, who was always very fearful of his father.

Usually dysfunctional families avoid having house guests, especially overnight guests. So we never stayed overnight at Annie's home. The entire family was rather reclusive. From what I was told, it wasn't always that way. Back in the late 1960s and early 1970s while Mr. Chen was working toward his PhD, they had friends and were social. It was only after he gave up that quest and went to work at Texas Instruments that he started showing bursts of temper.

Despite her tense, unhappy home environment, Annie was a good student all through school. Not that this is news to any first-generation Taiwanese-American. From the time you can walk and talk it is ingrained in your brain that you have to excel in school. That supersedes anything else. You have a miserable home life? Too bad. You have to excel in school to excel in life, and that's that. Annie knew that, and I knew that, and every other Taiwanese kid we met knew that. It is a cultural bedrock. The demand for academic excellence is pervasive in Chinese culture. Straight As and nothing else.

Our families got together every month or month and a half, starting in January 1978, and continued through my middle-school years, high school, and into college until June 1986, when I got married. After that my family continued their visits without me.

Annie did her undergraduate studies at Yale and is a graduate of Harvard Law School. For about ten years, she has been teaching law at American University in Washington, DC, where her main focus is human trafficking.

Annie got married in her mid-thirties, which is very late for our culture. She lives in a Washington, DC, suburb with her Caucasian husband, Daniel, and two sons, born in 2009 and 2011 respectively. Daniel is an associate at a law firm.

It's interesting to me that of my three Taiwanese friends from childhood, I got married first when I was just twenty. Everyone else waited until their thirties. Mary was pushing forty. Just like with Pat, Annie's and Mary's parents constantly meddled in their choice of boyfriends while trying to play matchmaker. I never gave my parents the chance.

Annie met Daniel through work, but I wouldn't call it a love match. Like Pat and Mary, her decision to marry was driven by practicality more than romance. Also, I have no doubt she was desperate to quiet her mother's nagging. I had known Mrs. Chen most of my life and could just imagine her nattering at Annie in Taiwanese: *You need to hurry up and find a husband. You're getting too old. It's getting too late to have children. Why can't you find a suitable husband?*

Being a little older both Annie and Daniel were financially secure as working attorneys in their respective fields. So they had a very American-style destination wedding in Napa, California, meaning all the relatives and guests had to make their own way there. They rented out a venue that did all the ceremony and reception preparations for them.

It was a typical western wedding: the bride wore a white dress and stayed in it throughout the ceremony and reception. There was no Chinese ceremony with the requisite red dress and formal multi-course dinner. Annie and Daniel's reception was a party, an extravaganza that had to cost tens of thousands of dollars. The couple paid for it themselves; their parents were not asked to contribute nor did their families have any say in either the ceremony or reception.

There was no shame attached to Annie marrying Daniel. But you could tell her parents thought he was meh. He had a steady career but wasn't a standout. Annie's family considered her more successful than her husband. On the other hand, Annie's parents were just so relieved she had finally married anybody. As long as he was fertile, they'd live with it because in their eyes she had no time to waste. She needed to get pregnant immediately. And she pretty much did and had two very cute and smart brown-haired boys.

I also find it interesting that all of my three Taiwanese friends grew up to be very independent and determined not to be in anyone's shadow. To that end, none of them took their husband's name. I've noticed that among American professional couples, a woman may be called Dr. Patricia Smith, but when referring to a couple it's Mr. and Mrs. Jones. Or the names might be hyphenated. But none of my childhood friends had hyphenated surnames and no Mr. and Mrs. So-and-so for them. So when I sent out Christmas cards, I would address it Dr. Jane Chen and family.

On the other hand, my father was unhappy that I took my husband's last name. Kind of. When William and I first met, we were both amused that we shared the same last name: Hwang for him and Huang for me. But it's not as much of a coincidence as you might think. Huang is one of the most common surnames in China, with about thirty million people sharing the name. It's also an old name, tracing back more than 4,200 years. Huang is a variant of Hwang; it's like going from Gonzalez to Gonzales.

The reason for the different spelling? We have Immigration to thank. The official who processed my family spelled the name with a U; the one who admitted my husband's family chose W. Throughout American history, many immigrants' names were changed as they were processed through Ellis Island and other entry spots, and once the new spelling is on your official documents, that's what you went with.

But in reality, it is essentially the same name, the same Chinese character, with the same meaning: yellow, as in the color. Didn't matter. My father protested and tried to dissuade me. I think the reason he made such a big deal about it had less to do with family pride than his upset that his nineteen-year-old daughter was marrying a virtual stranger and had not seen fit to ask his permission. Or even let him meet the guy. More on that later.

When it came to raising their kids, Annie and Daniel

were very amicable. And as they were both busy professionals, the kids were supervised primarily by a nanny. And the kids seemed to be thriving. Together they seemed comfortable as a couple but whether it was a happy marriage, I guess would depend on what they were each looking for. And that is something only the people involved know.

In Taiwanese culture, as I've mentioned, it is not encouraged to wear your heart on your sleeve. It is considered almost a sign of weakness. So everything is kept inside. That in turn creates simmering resentments, which undermines the relationship—you can't work things out if you don't talk about them. I've often wondered if this cultural reticence is the reason the divorce rate in Taiwan is so high. Statistically, it's twice as high as in the United States. Other Asian countries are seeing similarly high relative divorce rates.

I remember reading an article reporting in the *Taipei Times* newspaper how women in Taiwan remain "unconvinced" by marriage. It talked of how unhappy marriages abounded throughout the island and that Taiwan leads industrialized Asia in divorce.

So much for getting married on a lucky day.

The article reported that more than half of women polled said they would not be happier if they were married, and only 39.5 percent thought married people were happier than those who stayed single. Apparently the issue of women not getting married was becoming a trend throughout East and South East Asia.

A funny sidebar to this was how Taiwanese men were responding to the dwindling number of women wanting to get married: "mail order" foreign brides. According to a paper titled *Gender Imbalances and the Twisted Marriage Market in Taiwan:*

Due to the immigration of foreign brides to Taiwan, the number of men who face the marriage squeeze problem has greatly declined, and for them the problem appears solved. But this has placed women in a similar predicament, which appears to be worsening, especially for women with lower education, living in rural areas, or belonging to the lower classes, with less opportunity for upward mobility. We argue that this problem will get worse if the foreign brides keep entering Taiwan. In the near future, Taiwanese males will have better spousal availability in the marriage market as the situation unexpectedly changes to a surplus of marriageable women. This will affect females' possibility of finding a marriage partner in the Taiwan marriage market.

What's most remarkable about Taiwanese men seeking foreign brides is that from a woman's perspective, most Taiwanese parents are emphatic that their daughters marry another Taiwanese or at the very least another Asian. That is on top of the general pressure to get married. For most Americans, while their parents might be eager for their children to get married, they don't really have a say in it. American young adults love their parents, but there's not really the same pressure for obedience.

Both Annie and I were raised with a strong sense of obligation that can be hard to ignore. Part of you grows up striving to please them—especially in academics. That makes it hard to spread your wings and become an independent adult making your own decisions. Even when you're married with kids, it can be a struggle not to automatically do what your mother says and what your father expects. It's not love they expect; it's loyalty. And that expectation is typical of our culture. We feel forever indebted to our parents in part because of the sacrifices they made coming to the United States. I'm not so sure my father's reason for coming to America was necessarily to make a better life for his children, but the end result was the same.

None of our group of immigrant daughters followed in our mother's footsteps of staying in the shadow so their husbands could succeed. Each of us was very ambitious. Personally, I can't imagine being my mother, completely subjugating my dreams and ambitions so my father could continue his indulgent pursuit of a doctorate.

My friends' mothers were very similar to mine. None of them advanced themselves in the United States. If their mothers worked at all, it was at some type of semi-skilled work like clerical tasks or keypunching. But their generation of Taiwanese women took a backseat to their husbands, so I identified much more with my father than with my mother because I was goal-oriented.

By contrast all of our fathers were driven, in one way or another. First, they left what they felt was political op-pression in Taiwan, knowing they would be persecuted if they did not join and announce allegiance to the KMT. They made genuine sacrifices leaving Taiwan knowing they could have no contact with their families until they had earned their American graduate degrees. Even so that shouldn't have meant that only their goals counted or were important.

力

I found it curious that when I visited Annie in 2015, she kept it a secret from her mother. There we were, grown women in our forties, and her mother wouldn't approve of us getting together. She also apparently didn't want anything to do with anyone from my family. I don't know if there was a falling out I didn't know about, or if it was just part of whatever ailed her. I didn't take it personally, though. Her mother apparently behaved that way toward pretty much everyone Annie knew. It wasn't a Taiwanese or cultural thing. It was a Mrs. Chen thing. Over the years she had withdrawn from any social life, isolating herself. I wondered if she suffered from depression or a type of dementia. Mr. Chen had mellowed a lot since his door-busting days and no longer displayed such a fiery temperament. But their marriage seemed very distant. I couldn't imagine being that miserable and just accepting it. And it wasn't like divorce was taboo in Taiwanese culture. But for some reason the Chens stayed together. I know people say they stay together for the kids, but I'm not so sure living in a tense, anger-filled home did Annie and her brother any favors. And that would be true regardless of their cultural background.

7

MARY

I met Mary in 1978 after my father had received his acceptance to start his PhD at Texas A&M. Her father had just finished his PhD in forestry at College Station and was looking for a job. Considering that every other Taiwanese I knew seemed to be in mathematics or some hard science field of study, forestry seemed a curious, almost exotic choice for a career, especially since Mary's father was a chemistry major in Taiwan. Of course, that had not been his choice; he was told what career he could pursue. Those who scored the highest on their college entrance exams were automatically eligible for medical school and could begin by getting pre-med undergraduate degrees. Those in the second tier of scores studied engineering. And those with lower rankings were relegated to literature and liberal arts.

Mary's family had come to the United States during the 1960s like we had, and the two of us were close in age. Her father had wanted to become a doctor, but his exam score put that field out of his reach. Same with my

90

father, who more than once wistfully commented that if he'd only scored a few points higher on his exam, he could have qualified for medical school. The impression I grew up with of my father was someone who never finished what he started. But perhaps if he had been allowed to pursue his true passion, his life would have taken a much different path.

When Mary's father got to College Station, he chose forestry, allegedly thinking that it was close to his original field of study, chemistry. Not sure if that was simply his excuse to avoid a career in a field he had no interest in or this educated man genuinely thought forestry and chemistry were comparable careers. One thing I do know is that years later he took serious vicarious pleasure in Mary becoming a medical doctor.

Anyway, our fathers met at one of the anti-KMT events we would attend, and they had enough in common—both Taiwanese, both anti-KMT, and both somewhat isolated from their peers at the college—that they struck up a friendship. But they were very different personalities, and I wondered if they would have been friends had they met back in Taiwan.

What was nice about visiting Mary's family is that they lived in the same town as we did, so there were no hours-long commutes. But our families' times together would be brief. They moved to Wisconsin after Mary's father got a good job in forestry, a job he kept for more than twenty years. He provided his family a stable, middle-class life, which was in sharp contrast to my nomadic childhood living in projects and campus housing.

When they were getting ready to move, Mary needed someone to take care of her goldfish, so she asked me. Ever-so-slightly panicked, I told her I didn't know anything about goldfish—the last thing I wanted was to kill her pet. So she showed me how to feed and take care of it including changing the filters and keeping the water fresh. I adopted the fish—I do not remember its name—and brought the aquarium to our one-bedroom apartment.

Once she was settled in Wisconsin, Mary and I started writing each other. I would always give her updates on the goldfish's well-being. It had to be one of the longest-living goldfish on record because it lived for years after she left. I was just as diligent writing Mary as I was Pat. It's curious how as kids we probably communicated much more in our letters than we ever had face-to-face.

Like Pat, Annie, and me, Mary was comfortable integrating into her American life. During middle school she informed her parents that their Chinese names were very difficult for Americans to pronounce and took it upon herself to give her whole family Anglo names. She chose Mary for herself. She called her father George, an homage to the Curious George books she had read growing up. She dubbed her mother Marian, because it was a little like Mary. And her younger brother was the very all-American sounding Johnny.

For a family of Taiwanese immigrants, changing names was very informal. The family didn't go to a courthouse to fill out forms. They just adopted the new names and started using them even though their driver's licenses and other official documents still listed their Chinese names.

Mary did her undergraduate work at Harvard and then went to medical school at Yale. She became an oncologist and has lived in California since about 2006. For her it was all about school then all about her career, so she was still unmarried at forty-one, to her mother's intense dismay. And it wasn't because Mary was some shy wall-flower or unappealing. She is very attractive and vivacious. Marriage simply wasn't high on her bucket list.

When Mary was younger, her mother constantly complained how none of her boyfriends measured up: they were either too short, Caucasian, Cantonese, or Jewish—a typical Taiwanese mother's lament—so not one met the mother's approval. What a difference a couple of decades make. By the time Mary was on the downslope to forty, any pretense of gene pool pickiness from her mother was long gone. She was so desperate, she really didn't care who her daughter married. So Mary married a Caucasian man who worked for a telecommunication company. He had a master's degree, but by Mary's parents' standards was not nearly as successful as Mary was.

Again, it was not a case of love at first sight with Mary and her husband. They had been dating on and off for years, mostly because—at least from the outside—it appeared they didn't want the same things. Finally, after they had started seeing each other yet again for the fourth time, he finally gave Mary an ultimatum: *I'm getting older. I want to have a family; I want to have kids. If you don't want to continue dating, then this is our last breakup, and I'm going to move on and find someone else to marry. My clock is ticking.*

Mary acquiesced. She told me her response was: "Okay, okay, okay. I'll marry you."

When I found out that her husband had been married before, I was surprised her parents hadn't threatened to disown her over it. When I asked her about it, Mary sighed. "You know, at that point, I was over forty years old, and they were so desperate for me to finally get married that literally anybody would do."

Mary underwent in vitro fertilization and when she

was forty-two gave birth to twins. So that box was checked off. But it was not a warm and fuzzy relationship. They seemed to argue constantly, even in front of friends, which is not the way of most Taiwanese. Once when I was visiting Mary and we went to dinner, she did not want to sit next to her husband, as if even being in close physical proximity was unpleasant.

And yet in other ways she adhered to long-held Taiwanese traditions, such as personal matters like disease are very private. Even common afflictions. One of my favorite professional events is giving commencement speeches, like this one I gave at the University of Texas Health Science Center at San Antonio (UTHSCSA) School of Medicine.

> May I be the first fellow alum to address you as doctor.
>
> It was nearly a quarter century ago that I sat in those seats on a day like this. I was very proud, as you all should be right now. Finally, I was receiving that Doctor of Medicine degree and that hard-earned diploma. For me this ceremony was especially significant because up until that day, I only had a high school diploma. I started school here after three years of undergraduate studies.
>
> You've worn your white coats since your first semester. Today, you'll put away your waist-length white coats because your new ones will extend all the way down below your knees. That's a mark of growth!
>
> And that long white coat symbolizes the power of knowledge you've acquired here with the responsibility to go out into this world and heal people, in whichever specialty you choose.

At such a moment, it's natural to feel invincible. From my point of view as a child and adolescent psychiatrist, I've seen many teenagers wearing these cloaks of invincibility. They're young and strong, and they're sure they can do just about anything and not get harmed.

Likewise, medical education gives us doctors the enormous power to heal people, our patients. But what I realized during my career is that no matter how much knowledge you've gained or how skillful your hands—even if you become the best surgeon—you just can't escape being human. We doctors are not machines. We might seem and feel superhuman at times, but we are more human than not.

Sadly, doctors often fail to take care of their own bodies and then try to heal others. The truth is that we can succumb to the same diseases and illnesses as our patients, and we might even end up worse than those we treat.

For me, it happened early on and caught me by surprise. During my fellowship I went to the university clinic one afternoon because my eyes were getting itchy and inflamed, which I attributed to allergies. I was first seen by the resident, then fellow, then when the faculty attending physician examined me even more thoroughly I sensed from his body language that this was more serious. I was diagnosed with glaucoma and treatment started immediately.

I thought this was a disease that old people get. I was only twenty-nine years old.

A few years ago, my knuckles and fingers began to swell, and then I couldn't remove my ring when I was washing my hands. There was swelling in my other joints as well. On a blood draw, we found elevated levels of anti-CCP (a specific marker), positive rheumatoid factor, and elevated sed rate.[2] Since the onset had been slow and once again insidious, I didn't know I had rheumatoid arthritis.

So two chronic illnesses, no cure for either, but with daily medications for treatment, my symptoms have not worsened.

What saddens me the most is that some of my classmates with whom I shared lecture halls and gross anatomy lab, those who sat next to me during all these classes, have died before their time. What a terrible shame to spend all these years in medical school, learning about our bodies, and then we don't even take care of our own bodies.

Doctors, we are not invincible. We must take the time to take care of ourselves because you can't effectively take care of others if you neglect yourself.

Still, there are times when physical treatment doesn't solve the ailment. Through the years I have come across illnesses that cannot be healed physically. Human suffering causes our minds to generate feelings of anger, fear, and pain. Regardless of what happens to the body, true healing takes place in the mind, the calming effects of healing our souls. As a physician, wife, mother of two sons, and an immigrant, I have always had to overcome adversity. I have found healing through writing, now authoring two autobiographical books and a third book in progress.

You are here to heal, and you are your most

---

[2] A sedimentation rate, also called a sed rate, is a blood test which detects non-specific inflammation. It is typically ordered when a doctor suspects arthritis.

important patient. Be vigilant about your own health first. And when you sense you have a problem, embrace it because it will make you a better healer.

My fellow doctors, my message to you: heal thyself first, so you can heal others.

Talking about my battle with rheumatoid arthritis (RA) to anyone would be considered a bit scandalous by my relatives back in Taiwan. So you can imagine how not thrilled my parents were that I aired personal business in front of an auditorium full of complete strangers. Mary might not have thought too much about my RA disclosure, but she was stunned when she read the white coat speech I planned to give in July 2015, also at UTHSCSA. I'd been asked to speak at several white coat ceremonies, which is for when the incoming first-year medical students are presented with their white medical coat. It's a big deal. What made this particular event special was that my own son would be in that group of 220 medical students.

I had emailed her the speech a week before the ceremony, and a few days later we met up. Once we were face-to-face, she immediately asked, "Are you really going to give that speech?"

"Of course."

"And your father and mother are going to be in the audience?"

I confirmed they were. Although my father's facial expression wouldn't give away his thoughts or feelings, his body would be tense. My mother, on the other hand, wouldn't understand since she still essentially did not speak English. But my father would tell her what was said after the fact.

"They're going to disown you," Mary predicted.

It was actually a possibility. Or more likely, as Mary added, "They're going to call you up and rant and rave for the next month."

I shrugged but I understood Mary's reaction. There are some things in our traditional culture you just don't do.

Thank you for inviting me to be part of this special day. It's an honor to be here with all of you.

My, what a fine-looking group of young men and women. And smart, too. Well, you can't beat that combination. Welcome, entering medical class of 2019.

It was not so long ago that I sat in those same seats on a day like this. Well, actually, it was almost three decades ago. Among those sitting with you right now, someone will become your best friend. Someone else might become your maid of honor, best man, or maybe even your husband or wife. Your future practice partner might be sitting near you today.

For me, I came here to get my MD. Well, that happened. Unexpectedly, I also ended up getting my Mrs.—to another medical student at this school. And sometime after that, a baby, too. Yes, all right here.

The truth is things don't always go as planned. I had set my sights on becoming an ER doctor because I was drawn to the drama and intensity, the excitement.

You see, my family made lots of trips to the emergency room—much like university hospital and the Robert B. Green—and since my parents didn't speak English well, I was the family spokesperson. *My little brother almost sliced off his finger,* I would say to the triage nurse. *My baby sister has a fever.*

One night when my baby sister was two and a

half, she started convulsing, so we rushed to the ER. That night she was diagnosed with acute lymphocytic leukemia.

Doctors told us that she couldn't be cured; they could only prolong her life. Back in the '70s, there were no protocols for treating leukemia. So my little sister went through clinical trials, not knowing if these treatments—a cocktail mixture of chemo and radiation—would save her life or would kill her.

I went into the exam rooms and watched her go through these and other traumatic procedures including painful bone marrow aspirations with a huge metal tube stuck into her hip. And that's when I decided to become a doctor and help people. I was eleven years old.

So actually my dying sister inspired me to become a doctor.

During my second year of school here, I got a phone call from my brother who found her dead. She was thirteen years old. My little sister had died in her sleep. I was in shock and couldn't continue emotionally.

When life takes a sad, unexpected turn, it doesn't matter how smart you are or how caring. These cruel forces threw me off my feet. My thoughts were frozen, and I kept thinking back to my sister's body. Every time I heard an ambulance, I thought of her. I couldn't read or concentrate. Every time I saw a cadaver, I thought I saw my sister.

The same person who propelled me to go into medicine was the same figure who was holding me back; I couldn't continue because my grief was so overwhelming.

The associate dean for student affairs at the time granted me a leave of absence. And that was a pivotal moment in my life; I decided to become a psychiatrist. Having experienced first-hand someone dying, the searing pain of my sister dying so suddenly, I realized that psychiatry was my calling. And the truth was I had an edge over those who'd never experienced something so painful.

I've shared my personal story with you because you've chosen a challenging route. You never know what might happen along the way, so if something goes wrong, ask for help. Luckily you have chosen a remarkable medical school. The support of this school helped me through the death of the person who inspired me to go into medicine. So if you're not at the top of your class, don't worry about it. After all, only one person can be at the top of this class.

The unpredictable nature of life means that cruel forces can push you off your path unexpectedly. If that ever happens to you, don't, don't, please don't give up.

Remember, you're not alone in this great endeavor. Thank you, and my best wishes to all.

The taboo about diseases in general and cancer very much in particular is that Taiwanese believe it reflects badly on the family as a whole because it means you carry the cancer gene. That makes the following generations undesirable for marriage. And yes, some cancers do seem to have a genetic component, but it's complex and not necessarily a direct correlation like hemophilia. To me, knowledge is power. Keeping secrets about your family's medical history only opens the door for avoidable complications. It's not a reflection of who you are as a person or your value as an individual. But these kinds of cultural beliefs are hard to break.

Mary's response to my memoir, *Grown-Up Child*, was similar. After she read an early draft she commented how brave I was while I was at her house having dinner.

"Why was it brave to write a memoir?" her husband innocently asked.

He couldn't possibly understand the driving force shame was in most Asian cultures, and few things were more shameful than exposing your family secrets to the outside world.

When my parents found out that I had written a memoir of my early years, my mother said, "You can't publish it. You can't do that. It brings too much shame to all of us."

Both my parents were also adamant that I not publish my memoir because they worried that pro-KMT political thugs would come after me in fury. Mind you this is forty years after Chiang Kai-shek had died, but that was their thinking. They were so worried about angering authorities who didn't know who I was and didn't care. And they were appalled by the idea of opening up my life as easily as one would open a book.

So you can imagine how thrilled they were when the Fox Sports News website published an article about my annual participation in trying out for the Dallas Cowboys cheerleaders even though I'm a couple decades older than most of the participants and have zero dance background. The article came out over Thanksgiving and my parents were over for dinner. My father wanted to see the article so I printed out a copy. You know, to some degree all adult children have to deal with generational differences with their parents. Add to that the cultural differences when your parents are immigrants and the disconnects go up exponentially.

When my father saw the photos accompanying the feature, he blurted out in Taiwanese, "Oh, no! You're almost naked!"

Actually, I had on shorts and a short, cropped top. Your average aerobics instructor wears less. Yes, my navel was showing. Mind you, I was forty-nine at the time. I work out regularly to stay in shape in general but to get ready for the tryouts, I train like I'm doing an Iron Man as opposed to a sixty-second dance routine. My point being, I thought it was a good picture.

My mother ... not so much. She peered over my father's shoulder and her expression pinched with disapproval. She couldn't read the article since she had never learned the language, but she stared at the colored photos in the article and announced they were not appropriate. Then she asked if I got paid for the article and if not why not while my father remained fixated on my naked navel—until I casually asked my parents about what had happened to anti-Kuomintang activists during the '60s and '70s. They provided some information then my father asked why I wanted to know.

When I explained I wanted to write a book about the influence that the KMT had on Taiwanese immigrants in general, my (perceived) photographic immodesty was forgotten.

"No, you cannot write such a thing," he announced. "You're going to get death threats. They're going to come after you. You're putting your life in danger. You're putting *our* lives in danger."

I explained it was the follow-up book to the memoir I

had written of my early years as a daughter of immigrants. This time my mother nearly went apoplectic.

"You can't publish that. How can you expose such a personal thing?" she asked, no doubt thinking about my sister's illness. "It will bring too much shame to all of us."

So that argument went on a while, leading to tension the rest of the day. Apparently, some Thanksgiving traditions hold true regardless of where you're from.

I wasn't surprised by their reactions; I knew my writing aspirations would not be encouraged, so my feelings weren't hurt. Their primary concern was avoiding public shame over a child with cancer and me riling up the remnants of KMT thugs who by then didn't know who I was and wouldn't care. But their early years living under oppression had left an indelible, permanent mark.

Being raised by parents with a fundamentally different worldview, as all my Taiwanese childhood friends had been, created a host of culture clashes, especially if they married an American. It was a disconnect they never bridged, and it affected other aspects of their marriage, in Mary's case child-rearing particularly. Mary was strict, and her husband was lenient. She wanted to establish a set routine that incorporated discipline. But her husband disagreed completely; his attitude was: *Let them play. They're just kids.* He also believed their children should have the freedom to form their own ideas. Have a say in what they wanted to do. Have choices.

All of that was completely contradictory to Mary's philosophy of child-rearing, and to mine as well. I don't believe in a multiplicity of choices. My opinion is that two choices are sufficient for small children.

Mary's situation reminded me of a conversation I had once with an acquaintance of mine, Natalie, who is Vietnamese. She married an American and they were constantly at odds over parenting. Her son was about five years old when she commented, "The way we were brought up," meaning her and I, "was so straightforward: parents told the kids what to do, and we obeyed."

Or at least we didn't argue the point and found ways around it. Like getting engaged during a first date at nineteen. But I digress. By and large she was right.

Then she added, "It must be a lot easier for you than for me because your husband is Taiwanese." Meaning he too was raised with demanding parents. "I bet he backs you up when you set a rule. Mine constantly argues with me."

In that she was right; because we had been raised in the same culture, my husband and I did share similar parenting views, especially when it came to academic achievement and being respectful. In fact, he probably wouldn't have minded me being more strict. But there were also stark differences in how we raised our kids compared to how we were raised. How *I* was raised in particular; for one I never expected either of my kids to be the grown-up of the household. But again, I digress.

The bottom line was, Americans tended to believe in giving their kids more rope than a typical Asian family when it came to freedom of thought, expressing an unsolicited opinion, being more a master of their own destiny starting at a younger age. Americans believed in giving their kids space. That wasn't a concern among most Taiwanese parents I knew growing up. So my friends' mothers were always very involved in their lives and their choices—and expected their wishes to be met—even when they became adults. My mother probably would have liked that too, but I chose a different path, much to the surprise of those who knew me, including my friends. Instead of going to school, getting a degree, establishing a career, then getting married, I did things a little in reverse.

8

WHAT'S LOVE GOT TO DO WITH IT?

Of all the differences between American and Tai-wanese culture, perhaps none is more pronounced than attitudes about marriage. The majority of Americans want to marry for love. If a woman seeks out a husband strictly for financial security, she's considered a gold digger. In Taiwan she'd be considered practical.

Neither my parents nor the parents of the Taiwanese girls I knew growing up had romantic courtships. They were either set up by matchmakers or got married because they felt the pressure of age, time, expectations, and im-patient parents. None of our parents married for love. And neither did I. But I didn't get married because of some clock ticking. It was based on practicality and a bit of rebel-lion. I was the youngest in our group to get married, which is ironic because I would have definitely been voted least likely to get out from under their mother's thumb.

After Mary, Pat, and Annie graduated from high

school, all three of them went away to college. As in to a different city where they lived in dorms like normal college students with other girls their own age, were able to make friends, and experience some independence. After I graduated from high school at seventeen, my mother insisted I go to college locally and continue to live at home. My roommate was an elementary-school child—my little sister who was nine years younger. We shared the same bed, which was actually two foldout cots pushed together in a very small bedroom. To keep the flimsy mattresses from sagging, we propped them up with stacks of our father's textbooks.

Of course I loved my little sister, but I also wanted to start living my life. Other girls were growing up and reaching out. I was allowed to go to college, I could attend classes, but I was locked out of college life because of my mother's strict control. Money was not the problem; I had Pell grants, scholarships, and other sources of assistance to pay all of my room and board in addition to tuition and other college expenses. None of that mattered because my mother wanted to retain her control over me.

Prior to my sophomore year I tried again. "I would like to live in a dorm on campus. This way, I'll get involved with more activities. Living at home I miss out on a lot of what's going on. And it will help me with medical school. I'll get to meet more people."

My mother was adamant and refused. I thought I was going to go crazy. No other pre-med college student I knew had a mother who was there waiting to drive me home the second my classes were over. It was suffocating.

So when I was a junior, for the first time in my life, I directly defied her. Behind her back I transferred to the University of Texas at Austin for my remaining undergraduate semester. The application involved a lot of detailed work, with mail going back and forth. To keep my mother from intercepting any of the correspondence, I rented a PO box on the A&M campus. After I was accepted, I then applied to get into a dorm. At the time it was a challenge because freshmen got priority, but they had private dorms to accommodate the overflow. I finally got a dorm assignment a week before school started. My mother was infuriated, but I didn't care. I was out of the house and felt free. Kind of. Even though I was one hundred miles from home, at times I felt I might as well still be living in the family apartment. She phoned me constantly and kept sending me their bills to pay and mail to answer.

But all that became a secondary concern when I was accepted by the University of Texas Health Science Center School of Medicine. I was nineteen years old and truly felt the world was my oyster. Okay, at the time I didn't really understand what that phrase meant, but it sounded like I felt.

On Martin Luther King weekend, Katie, one of my college friends, dropped me off at the bus station. I took a Greyhound eighty miles to San Antonio so I could spend the day looking for an apartment. Katie also offered to pick me up when I returned the next evening. I would have never believed how everything would change in that twenty-four hours.

While in San Antonio, I stayed with a friend who was going to college there, and she introduced me to a few other students including William, a twenty-five-year-old, first-year medical student, who had also been born in Taiwan.

"Want to go out to eat after you look for an apartment?" he asked.

I said sure. Although his demeanor was casual, it held

some significance for me—it was the first date I'd ever been on. At dinner I found out he'd been in the United States since he was seventeen. We spoke English to one another even though he's not very fluent. But we didn't have a long time to converse because as soon as we finished eating, he pointed out the window toward a movie theatre complex across the street.

"Want to go see what's playing?"

Again, I immediately agreed. It was a day of firsts; I'd never been to a movie theatre before. It did briefly occur to me I was going off with some man I did not know at all. For all I knew he could be pro-KMT or Mandarin. But I felt comfortable. And I wanted to see a movie. Inside the theatre I followed the cue of others. After buying tickets everyone seemed to head straight for the snack bar. While William bought us a large popcorn and a soda, I took in the bright, colorful multiplex decorated with film posters and lots of neon. It was magical.

We went into one of the theatres and found some seats. The chair reclined, and I was surprised at how comfortable it was. And how big. They were wide enough for two of me. After a series of trailers for upcoming films, the movie started. It was *Out of Africa* starring Meryl Streep and Robert Redford and was based on Karen Blixen's memoir of the same name about her time living in Africa. The sound system was so amazing—I was used to listening to an old transistor radio—I could feel the vibration go through me. And the detail on the screen was mesmerizing. I had to contain my excitement so I didn't look like an idiot. William and I sat side-by-side watching the movie, careful to avoid inadvertent touching, sharing the popcorn and soda. It was the most fun I'd ever had in my life.

After it was over we left the theatre and were walking

to nowhere in particular, talking about the Meryl Streep character. William was walking next to me but not too close. Nor did he offer his arm or try to take my hand. Even casual public displays of affection are not the Asian way in particular or the Taiwanese way in particular. And that's as true for married couples as it is two people on a first date.

All those times we visited the other Taiwanese families as a kid, I have never once witnessed the slightest gesture of affection between my friends' parents. And since we didn't see our parents displaying any affection, we all carry on that taboo of touching in public. So I would have been shocked had he tried to hold my hand or make some other gesture of affection.

Instead, he surprised me another way. After a brief lull in the conversation, he said, "Let's get married."

His tone was so nonchalant; he could have been suggesting we go get some ice cream.

I didn't respond right away. Not because I was trying to figure out how to politely decline—my decision to accept his proposal was unequivocal and instantaneous—but because I was figuring out what dates would work. I've always been extremely organized and used to write everything down in a notebook-size Day-Timer personal calendar and was mentally flipping pages. It would have to be on a Saturday, it had to be after I finished my undergraduate studies, and it had to be before medical school started in August. While I narrowed down the timeframe, William waited patiently, not at all nervous. Finally, I gave him two dates to choose from: July 19 or July 26. We settled on July 19.

William walked me back to my friend's building and politely said goodnight, the way a study partner would.

There was no kiss, no hug, no twinkle in his eyes. There was no flirtation from either of us. Or shyness for that matter. My heart didn't skip a beat nor was my head in the clouds. We exchanged phone numbers, and he left.

That night my mind wouldn't shut down, and I couldn't sleep. Maybe for a nanosecond I asked myself what I was thinking saying I would marry a complete stranger, but the doubt was short-lived. I definitely wanted to get married, and he had simply made me an offer I couldn't refuse. I wasn't excited as much as I was relieved at knowing I was cutting the ties that kept me tethered to my mother, so I could live the life I wanted to have. She wouldn't be able to dominate me—at least not as much as if I stayed single. And an added bonus: I wouldn't have to endure her trying to act as my matchmaker or finding fault when I started dating like my Taiwanese friends suffered through.

He's an engineer? What, with only a master's degree? Not acceptable!

He's a doctor? What kind? Family practice? No, not good enough. Find a surgeon or specialist instead.

There would have been no end to that dialog until I had done what they wanted. William's proposal had spared me all that. And I think the reason he proposed so very fast, even though he didn't know me, was simply that he was lonely and wanted a wife.

We were what the other needed.

Obviously, at that point I certainly didn't love him, but I did have a sense about him. From just our short time together that night he was obviously very driven. Sure, he was also good-looking, intelligent, educated, Taiwanese, the right age, and in med school—good husband and father material. But his ambition and drive were appealing. He was clearly confident of himself and a fast decision-maker.

In short, he was the antithesis of my father. Sure, my father was ambitious, but he didn't have perseverance or the drive to see things through when they got difficult. He was a procrastinator, and he waffled, hating to make a decision. I couldn't even count on him to remember to pick me up from school as a kid. So William's quiet decisiveness appealed to me, and I found it so refreshing to meet a man who had so many qualities my father lacked.

So I was nineteen with a wedding date although it wasn't the romantic occasion it is for most American young women. I didn't think of William as my fiancé or even my boyfriend—a term I would never use. I simply thought of him as the man I was getting married to.

力

On Sunday I returned to Austin from San Antonio, and Katie picked me up from the bus station.

"Did you find an apartment?" she asked on our way back to the car.

"I did. And I'm getting married!"

She stopped and stared. "You don't even have a boyfriend."

"I still don't. But a med student I met asked me to marry him, and I said yes."

"People don't do that here."

Katie was Mandarin, so she knew how it was. "What did your parents say?"

My silence told her I hadn't told them. No need to rush into that hurricane. But I happily told everyone else. On Monday in class I announced to anyone within hearing distance that I was getting married. Several commented they weren't aware I was dating anyone. I enjoyed their confused expressions when I confirmed I hadn't been.

After a week of procrastination, I called my mother and told her. "I need you to block out Saturday, July 19."

"Why?"

"I'm getting married."

It went downhill from there. Both of my parents argued, protested, fumed, and tried to categorically forbid me to marry anybody. I was too young. I didn't know William. *They* didn't know William. Then they decided I must be pregnant. I assured them that would only be possible through the second immaculate conception.

Then they switched their inquisition to William, and of course I couldn't answer the majority of their questions because I had only just met him myself. The most important nugget I could provide: he was going to be a doctor. Taiwanese parents don't say no if the prospect is a doctor. But they were still largely angry and against the marriage.

"When are we going to meet this man?" my mother demanded.

I checked my Day-Timer. "Probably around March during spring break," I said, then quickly hung up.

They weren't the only unhappy parents. I found out later that when William told his mother and father he was marrying a teenager he'd just met—I'd be twenty by the time we married—they were utterly shocked and strenuously disapproved for much the same reasons my parents itemized. It's the wrong timing. I'm too young. They don't know me. He doesn't know me. I don't know him. What was especially frustrating for them was they lived in California; they're too far away to have much control over him. It's easier to defy parents over the phone.

It was about a month after our first and only date that William and I saw each other again. Again, no sparks flew, and there was that same comfort level that I had made the right decision.

力

For a short while my pending marriage was not brought up by my parents; perhaps they thought by ignoring the subject it would go away. And I was happy to leave the elephant in the room alone. But the silence didn't last long, and in the months leading up to the wedding, all four parents tried every argument and strategy to persuade us not to get married. By June it was getting very heated. But I was busy planning the wedding, so I simply blocked most of the noise out.

On one hand organizing our ceremony and reception was in my comfort zone as far as being good with handling tasks. But I was out of my element when it came to the traditions of a wedding, especially since ours would blend both American and Taiwanese culture. So I asked for help from two friends: Michele, a Caucasian friend from College Station, Texas, who was my maid of honor, and Mary, now living in Madison, Wisconsin, who agreed to be my bridesmaid.

They'd both been shocked when I called and announced: *I need you to help with my wedding.* After answering the now-expected litany of questions, the ladies got down to wedding business.

"What are your colors?" Michele asked.

It was news to me that weddings had theme colors. I asked her to help me choose a color and we decided on lavender. Michele then offered to coordinate the dresses with

Mary, whom she'd never met. I gave her Mary's number, and they coordinated everything on the phone.

About a month before our wedding date, we officially got engaged just to say we did. Today you hear about elaborate surprise scenarios to make the proposal an event. Not us. We went out to dinner. There was no bended knee, no witnesses to our promises. But I felt it was a box that needed to be checked. Along with picking out my dresses. Yes, plural. A white one for the Christian portion of my ceremony, a red one for the reception. As I've mentioned, red is the color of good luck in Chinese culture.

In high school I'd never had a prom dress because I was never allowed to go to the prom. So when my mother offered to pay for my white wedding gown, I agreed, thinking it would even things out. We went to Bride 'n Formal, a discount chain store that specialized in prom dresses and bridal gowns. The store was in a washed-out strip mall, but I didn't care. Inside, the shop was a startlingly colorful environment, with racks crammed full of pastel dresses and gowns in every size and style—bouffant, strapless, spaghetti straps, brocaded, sequined—everything. It was late spring with prom season approaching.

The saleslady stared at me oddly, probably because I still looked about twelve—I'm a tick under five feet tall, 115 pounds, with a baby face. But any concerns she might have had about me being a potential underaged foreign mail order bride were eased the moment I started talking. Only someone raised in the South would have an accent like mine.

My mother helped me pick out a gown that was discounted to $40. She found the dress in the back of the store on a special sales rack. Minor problem: it was a women's size 12 and was big enough for me, plus my mother and

Mary to all fit in. But altering sprawling wedding gowns by hand was not a difficult task for my mother. After a couple of hours of work, my mother had slimmed down the huge dress to a beautiful wedding gown that fit me perfectly and looked exquisite. She also fashioned a lacy headpiece.

Looking back, I think that our do-it-yourself, economical approach to wedding dresses was about right. With our tiny budget, we had no choice. But I personally think that women make too big a deal about their wedding dresses, spending many thousands of dollars on a designer gown they'll only wear once for a few hours. The important thing is the marriage, not the packaging. In fact, after the wedding I sold my dress to a consignment shop specializing in wedding dresses and formals. I made someone happy, and I pocketed the change, which was actually more than the purchase price. Win-win.

Some of my friends were a bit taken aback that I turned around and sold the dress. But to me, being sentimental is for persons, not for things.

As I mentioned earlier, white in Chinese culture is associated with mourning. But we were getting married in the United States, where the first-time bride wears white. Even in Taiwan, women will wear white bridal gowns then change into traditional red Chinese dresses. Somewhere my mother found a red Chinese dress for me. Mind you, even while she was altering my gown and finding the red dress, she was still angry about and opposed to the wedding. So an undercurrent of tension was always present.

My mother had also come with me to buy the rings. There was a discount jewelry store in a new mall that had just opened in College Station, and they offered a three-for-one deal: matching his-and-hers wedding rings plus an engagement ring. It was perfect; one-stop shopping at an affordable price.

力

It's Chinese tradition to get married at the groom's home, and his parents lived outside of Los Angeles. The location was a traditional Protestant church where we had the Christian ceremony. After that we changed outfits: white bridal gown off, red Chinese gown with a high-neck collar on. The reception was at a Chinese restaurant, with dinner served banquet style, featuring about a dozen courses. All that was very customary for a Chinese wedding.

I didn't know any of the guests because they were all my husband's parents' people. It wasn't until two days before the wedding that Michele and Mary finally met my fiancé—and each other—after we all flew to Los Angeles. My family, friends, and I all stayed at the same motel, and when they arrived at the ceremony, Michele and Mary looked wonderful together in their beautiful lavender-themed dresses.

I still wouldn't call the wedding a particularly joyous occasion. It was strained. In the picture of my father walking me down the aisle, his grim face says it all. William's parents weren't any happier. But they all had to act cordial in front of the other guests.

力

We had a one-day honeymoon at Disneyland in Anaheim before flying back to Texas. The following Saturday we held a second reception in College Station for friends of my side of the family. About three hundred attended but the reception didn't cost us much at all. I was still officially a student at Texas A&M, and its Memorial Student Center has party rooms that can be reserved free of charge. All you have to pay for is the food you serve. We reserved an entire ballroom complete with tables and chairs, also free of charge. Then some of my parents' friends who owned mom-and-pop Chinese restaurants gave us a great deal on food, which we served on paper plates with plastic utensils. Nobody seemed to mind.

William and I were still in school, and I certainly couldn't count on my family helping us out, so the traditional money we received as wedding gifts—presented in special red envelopes—was very welcomed. I also registered at the local department stores for dishes, flatware, and household items. I didn't know that was something people did until a friend assured me it was an expected American custom. I didn't ask for a lot, just enough to get us started. Because I was such a wedding novice, I had no idea that I should do such a thing, but some friendly advice persuaded me to do that.

Had any KMT spies been around, our Texas reception could have been mistaken for a political gathering because most of my parents' friends and acquaintances were people they had met during the various anti-KMT rallies we had attended over the years. My mother was shocked that so many of them showed up. She didn't know I had invited them. But every year we would receive a directory from the association that put on the gatherings, so I sent the people I recognized an invitation. They had watched me grow up summer after summer, and apparently thought me getting married was a big deal, so they all showed up, red envelopes in hand.

In retrospect, the enthusiastic response was not

surprising. For these Taiwanese who had emigrated in the 1960s, their first-born children were all around my age, and I was the first member of my American-raised generation to get married. They turned out en masse, so our Texas reception ended up being quite the gathering.

While I wouldn't call the reception a party exactly, it even had entertainment. My sister—who had been delighted about my wedding—was in sixth grade. One of her classmates, a Chinese girl, was a very accomplished pianist and played a selection of classical pieces—from memory—at the reception. Free of charge, of course! In all, I doubt the reception cost me more than $50 in 1986 prices. And that includes the three-tier wedding cake, which I ordered from a local grocery store. If nothing else, growing up poor had taught me how to stretch a dollar.

On Sunday morning we cleaned the hall up, and that evening we headed to medical school and to the start of our married life. I didn't have a clue about the challenges ahead between a new marriage and my new status as a full-time medical student, but it wouldn't have mattered; I wouldn't have changed anything.

力

In the years since I've thought a lot about that spontaneous decision to get married to a complete stranger. I know part was to get away from my mother's dependency on me and her efforts to control my every move. Getting married would sever the tie once and for all. But it was more than that. William was so driven, such an obvious go-getter, that he inspired confidence and a sense of security I had never felt with my father. I loved my father, but I didn't trust him to take care of me.

Lastly, I sensed that we would be compatible, on a lot of levels. We would both be doctors, we were both ambitious, and both our families were Taiwanese immigrants, so we shared that cultural understanding. That was enough for me to say yes. And as I got to know William better in those early days of marriage and learned about his background and experiences, it turned out my instinct had been spot on, and I know without a doubt that the impulsive choice I made to marry a stranger that night in San Antonio was the best possible decision I could have ever made.

9

DOC

According to a couple of studies in 2017, couples in the United States, on average, date for about three years before getting engaged. Even thirty years ago, few Americans rushed into marriage. Clearly, I bucked that trend.

One thing about dating for years is that by the time you married, you would pretty much know your partner's life story from spending so much time together. But in my case, between the brevity of the engagement and living in different cities, I mostly just knew the main bullet points about my soon-to-be husband the day I showed up for the wedding—came to the United States when he was seventeen, was anti-Kuomintang, was ambitious, and came from what Americans would consider a middle-class family. It wouldn't be until later that I would find out the details and discover that while we obviously shared the same cultural background, his childhood was a world away from mine.

My worries as a kid mostly centered around being uprooted at a moment's notice because my father had fallen out of his latest PhD program. While the KMT spy under every bed paranoia that pervaded transplanted Taiwanese was a scary thought, it was abstract because nobody ever came and threatened us directly. And while they may have tried to intimidate my father's family by showing up to ask about his activities in the United States, none of his relatives ever disappeared. It was different for William because he grew up in Taiwan under the totalitarian regime.

William's grandparents had vivid memories of Taiwan when occupied by Japan and having to speak Japanese. Then after Japan lost World War II, among his grandparents and others, there was hope and excitement over Taiwan becoming independent. That was crushed when Chiang Kai-shek showed up. Anyone who spoke out too much against the KMT was likely put in front of a firing squad and executed. That put a damper on open dissent. But it didn't stamp it out completely. People just learned to keep their opinions private and become more subversive.

William was his parents' first born. Their next child, a girl, died in the mother's arms, which wasn't uncommon in the 1960s. Infant mortality back then was high. Their third child, also a daughter, had a lot of developmental problems related to the birth. A lot of doctors in Taiwan were trained in no pain childbirth, where the woman is given an epidural to help ease pain during labor.

In the 1960s most babies were born at home. I was, and so was William. But it was more dangerous. Not only was infant mortality high, but a lot of women also died during childbirth from hemorrhaging and other complications. After having their second child die, his parents decided they would find a specialist to deliver the third child. So William's mother went to the best hospital in Tainan City; it was a state-of-the-art facility.

At that time painless childbirth had started becoming a popular option. That's where the woman is given an epidural to help ease the discomfort during labor, especially long labors. But on occasion they would give the mother too much medication or give her an epidural too late in the process, making it difficult to push the baby out, and it would get stuck in the birth canal. So the doctor would use forceps or these suction devices to pull out the baby. A lot of kids in Taiwan, Japan, and Korea from that era have cerebral palsy as a result.

William said you could feel a deep dent in her head. She ended up severely handicapped, unable to really talk and had difficulty walking. So she can't speak, she slurs, she wobbles. She's severely handicapped. The family didn't care because she was alive. But she would be the object of scorn for others who would ridicule her or laugh at her. People were ignorant about handicaps and not very compassionate.

As a young man William's father went to the Taiwanese Presbyterian Seminary in Tainan City, which was well known for its support of Taiwanese independence and for retaining Taiwanese culture and language. Of course this meant they were very anti-KMT. The seminary would organize secret rallies attended by the local intelligentsia. His father carried on the tradition once he became a minister, and he passed his political views down to his son. When I met William, I had no idea how strong his political feelings were. But once started, he can talk passionately for a long time about the evils of the KMT because he had personally experienced martial law and the effects of the regime.

Between his father's political activities and trying to run his own ministry, he apparently wasn't around a lot for his family. Similar to my father, William was very close to his grandparents, who offered a secure, stable household. His parents' relationship was apparently not close. Some of William's earliest memories are of his mother taking him and his sister to a neighborhood near an Air Force base, where the houses were simple and made of wood. His mother was apparently romantically involved with a man who lived there, so she would drag the kids along when she went to see him. What was most confusing was that his mother insisted they call the man Daddy. Not a great memory for William.

His maternal grandparents owned a small café in Tainan that served simple food like smoothies and noodles. Looking back, he realizes this his grandparents were more like parents than his mother and father were and took care of him well into his teens.

In 1978, three years after Chiang Kai-shek died, Taiwan opened the door to immigration, and William's parents decided it was an opportune time to leave. Even if Chiang was gone and the KMT wasn't quite as powerful, they were still considered dangerous, so a lot of people wanted to get out. That was the official story he gave. There were other reasons, which William didn't find out about until many years later. William's father owed a lot of people a lot of money, including relatives. He had several outstanding loans, had failed in numerous businesses, and had trouble keeping a congregation. Pastors needed to be self-sufficient; the smaller the congregation, the smaller their income. So moving to the United States was the chance for a fresh start.

Before they could leave, though, they had to bribe some KMT officials so William could go with them. Because he was seventeen and male, he was close to the age where he would have to serve in the military, which was mandatory. My dad had served. He'd say that was where he learned how to smoke. They would hand out free cigarettes, and since there wasn't much to do, he started smoking. He didn't see any military action, so he felt it was a lot of wasted time.

For as excited as William was for the opportunities that awaited in the United States, it was also very bittersweet. Once he left, he wouldn't be able to come back, unless he wanted to go into the military. Which he didn't. So as the plane took off, William understood he might never see Taiwan again, and he never looked back.

力

Flash forward: In 2017 we took a family trip to Taiwan. It was our sons' and my idea. They were twenty-two and twenty-five and one was engaged so it would probably be the last time we traveled as a foursome. Plus, I think our sons had started getting a little curious about their heritage.

That was Doc's first time back since emigrating. It wasn't a happy homecoming. He experienced panic attacks, worried that the government would discover that he had not served his time in the military and not let him leave to go back to the United States. I pointed out that the KMT murder squads no longer existed. Plus you would have to establish residency in the country, which would mean staying for more than four months. And they didn't want people older than thirty-six anyway.

But again, the memory of oppression and the fear of having your life ruined was an emotional knee-jerk reaction for those who grew up under the KMT. Finally, around the third day Doc finally felt assured security people weren't going to come drag him away, and we were able to experience Taiwan as a family. Can't say our boys felt too much ancestral connection—they are American born and raised. But I still wanted them to have an awareness of the influences, struggles, and choices made that helped shape our family history.

力

Not long after settling into their new country, William continued his education, totally focused on becoming a doctor. The change of geography didn't do too much to change his father's fortunes though. He continued to work as a minister but didn't have his own church. He'd rent a room at a church on Sundays to hold a service but never developed a significant congregation. So he held a variety of jobs to try and supplement his income—as a banquet waiter, as a repairman, and selling cemetery plots to his congregation, which further drove people away. He never kept any job for very long.

Just like my father's unstable financial situation made me determined to be a success, the same was true for William. We'd later joke about how both of our fathers were such underachievers. I would tease William that at least my father only underachieved in one country; his father bombed out in two countries. But I do wonder if we'd have been as driven and ambitious if our fathers had been more successful at achieving their dreams.

One difference between our families was that both my parents, but especially my mother, held onto a fantasy that one day they would move back to Taiwan, where my father would get a job as a full-fledged professor. But William and his family were here to stay, so they didn't have a romanti-cized memory of Taiwan like my family did.

力

I grew up with one foot in each culture, and in my married life, I have sometimes found myself dealing with a similar dichotomy, although not with my husband. It's the expectations of others that can show how the culture of our parents can inform our perceptions as adults. I was reminded of this several years ago when my friend Mary was visiting me in Texas. We were in the car when my husband called.

I put the phone on speaker and answered, saying, "Hi, Doc."

Out of the corner of my eye, I saw Mary give me a strange look, but I just dismissed it, focusing on talking and driving in Dallas traffic.

I listened to whatever it was Doc needed to tell me, and then when he asked if I could do something for him, I automatically said, "Yes, sir; will do," which was my usual way of interacting with him. Actually, it's my way of dealing with almost everyone.

When I disconnected the call, Mary was still giving me that strange look that looked suspiciously like an angry glare.

"What?" I asked.

"You. Call. Him. *Sir?*" She was incredulous. "I can't believe you call him sir."

It was clear she thought I was being subservient, the way her mother had been subservient to her father. So from her perspective it seemed as if I was kowtowing. But saying *sir* and *ma'am* was automatic from being raised in the American South, where the words are common expressions of politeness and good manners. It didn't matter who you were talking to.

Mary and my other friends didn't grow up being looked after by Southerners who have their own code of what's proper. Even the ones who smoked and swore always said sir and ma'am—even to their parents. That had a big influence on me. Plus, being respectful is part of Taiwanese culture as well.

And as far as calling my husband Doc, that just kind of happened. Thinking back, we didn't really call each other by name. When we were in a group of people, we'd make eye contact and just spoke directly to one another. When we were alone, we didn't have to call each other anything because it was just the two of us and we knew who we were talking to. That went on for about the first fifteen years of our marriage.

Then one day we were at Charleston Airport back when our kids were in middle school and several planes were having mechanical issues—including ours—so we needed to get on a different flight. The airline counter was mobbed so William and I got into different lines to see which one would go faster. When it was clear mine was, I called out his name to get his attention. He didn't respond. Not so much as a twitch.

So the second time I said, "Hey, Doc." He turned immediately, which I thought was kind of funny. So since that day, he's always been Doc to me, and it feels perfectly normal.

力

If my parents had taught me anything, it was how I did not want to raise my own children. We would not live a transient life. We would not live in campus or public housing that was so small the kids had to sleep in the living room on cots. We would not subsist on welfare. We would not be isolated from peers, school friends, or neighbors. And my husband and I would not exist with a wall of passive-aggressive, resentful silence between us.

Doc and I had both, in our own way, lived a chaotic childhood and we were determined that would not be our new family's legacy. At the same time, we took the aspects of our upbringing we found beneficial—mental discipline and education. My father gave me math lessons regularly. Every night, he assigned me problems, and I did them. He promised to teach me more in the next chapter, and he always did. Then we would move on to the next textbook. Sometimes we went through two textbooks on the same topic, one after the other, so I would benefit from another publisher's point of view. I loved that constant regimen, and I thrived on it. That kind of training was valuable. That was how Doc and I had both been brought up.

Those math lessons were a home version of what children in Taiwan do as a matter of course. While growing up, my husband attended cram school every day after regular school. That extra tutoring helps students score high on tests to gain admission to better middle schools and high schools. In raising our own children, I implemented the same ideas. Fortunately, Doc and I had the same expectations for our kids and agreed on how to raise them. Admittedly, our standards were stricter than those of the typical Caucasian family, but we believed it was the best way for us.

We established a daily routine that stressed accomplishment and consistency. It was second nature for me to do that, and Doc backed me up. The entire time we were raising our two sons, who are now grown men in their twenties, we never actually sat down and planned our approach to parenting. My approach to parenting was my approach to life: you set a goal, and you carry it out. And it was instilled back as a child when I'd be given a set of math problems with the goal of learning how to figure out the correct answer so I could move to the next level.

That's what I did with my own children in whatever subjects I taught them. We sat down together, explained what their assignments were, then when they finished, went over their answers with them. Curious acquaintances and friends asked if tutoring my kids on advanced subjects at home would make them bored at school. If you have an inquisitive mind, you're never really bored. There are always new things to learn. So I kept doing what I was doing.

They always say one of the main things couples argue about is kids. But arguing about co-parenting just didn't happen in our home. Child-rearing was easy because we agreed on everything and we presented a unified front. And our kids excelled as expected. But unlike me, they also had social lives.

力

Even though Doc and I were of like minds when it came to child rearing and education, it took a long time for us to get to know each other because we had skipped the whole dating-to-get-to-know-you part. And more to the point, our instant marriage meant I had no time to get to know his family, either. I knew the basics, but it took a while to get the details. And to be honest, my first impressions weren't glowing. I found my father-in-law to be edgy, irritable, and aloof. Not exactly the personality traits you imagine a minister will have. He also had a volatile, hair-trigger temper.

Again, not a great fit for a minister. I found out later he went to the seminary after being unable to find success in any of his earlier business ventures. Put more bluntly, he couldn't hold down a job.

It was not a case of the apple not falling far from the tree. My father-in-law's father—Doc's paternal grandfather—had been ambitious and driven. His first wife, a midwife, had died childless. He then remarried and had two children with his second wife—their firstborn was Doc's father; the youngest was a girl.

Doc's grandfather worked as an elementary school teacher in Nanzhuang, a small town in northern Taiwan, then tested well enough to gain admission to medical school in Japan—there were no medical schools in Taiwan at the time. While there he became involved with another woman. After earning his degree he brought his Japanese mistress back to live in Nanzhuang despite still being married to his second wife, Doc's paternal grandmother. This was not uncommon in those days. And he ended up having seven more children with his mistress.

Perhaps that's why he died when he was only fifty-three. But I digress.

As the first-born son, my father-in-law inherited a sizeable inheritance from his father although he squandered all the money, mostly through failed business ventures. In Taiwan if you co-signed a deal and your partner bailed out, you'd be on the hook to pay all the creditors. Well, my father-in-law co-signed several deals where the main signer left Taiwan because they couldn't pay their bills, and my father-in-law was stuck with the debts. He just had a knack for picking unscrupulous people to do business with.

So when my in-laws arrived in the United States—they settled in the Los Angeles area—they did not have a financially stable life, just as my parents hadn't. He could never keep people in the congregation. It didn't help that my in-laws would get into arguments in front of the parishioners. And he was constantly moving the location of his services, often to dodgy areas where the rent was cheap. But his parishioners were mostly Chinese immigrants who were afraid of having what little they had stolen.

During the first twenty years of our marriage, my father-in-law must have moved his congregation a dozen times. Sometimes because he had a fight with the main preacher over the rent; other times he wasn't happy with the space provided. Occasionally there were complaints about the service itself. So he'd move the congregation to another rented space, often with little notice to the parish members. But he was just never satisfied; he was always unhappy with something. Each time he'd lose parishioners and then gain new ones—temporarily. I couldn't help but be reminded of my father. Both men had a kind of gypsy lifestyle that didn't include a whole lot of planning and contingencies.

No surprise that my father-in-law wasn't a big wage earner. But my mother-in-law was. She was pragmatic and had enrolled in beauty school as soon as they settled in the United States and worked in salons. Eventually she opened her own shop, a small facial studio, in Alhambra, a small city ten miles east of Los Angeles that is more than 50 percent Asian, so having a business where the workers spoke Taiwanese and Mandarin was a big selling point. Her clientele were mostly well-to-do Chinese who had immigrated in the 1980s and settled in California. Clearly Doc didn't take after his father when it came to ambition and business acumen. Doc actually attributes his success to watching his maternal grandfather work the noodle shop, manage the employees, and carefully count inventory of papayas, udon noodle stock, and soy milk.

My husband and I are irresistibly driven to succeed. All of our instincts lead us to make decisions toward that goal. It wasn't until fifteen or twenty years into our marriage that I realized that we had much more in common than I had ever thought. Our failure-prone fathers accounted for much of that. We are very alike in that way. Both of our fathers were impulsive and would practically jump up and move on the spur of the moment, not bothered by a single pragmatic thought.

I don't know if it was kismet or coincidence, but it is fascinating that Doc and I had so much in common—which we didn't really realize until long after we were married. We both had fathers pursuing an elusive academic goal causing us to grow up in somewhat insecure environments. Neither of our fathers was financially successful or personally fulfilled, and it deeply informed our own determination to succeed. I wonder if we somehow sensed we were kindred spirits that first night that ended with a proposal.

And I have to say it's worked out well. Although we have very different personalities—I'm the extrovert always willing to go on an adventure to try new things, while he's more reserved—we have proven to be very compatible. Just as with child-rearing, I did what I thought was right and figured that if Doc didn't like something, he would let me know.

力

Growing up it seemed like every kid I knew in the projects had stepparents, or half-siblings, or some combination of both because their parents had divorced at least once. But even though statistics show that there is a very high divorce rate in Taiwan, it's not something I have witnessed much among the immigrant families I know here in the United States. Maybe moving to a new country thousands of miles away from family acts as a kind of glue that makes people stay together even when unhappy. My parents and those of my Taiwanese childhood friends are all still together.

Maybe it's because they didn't get married because they were in love. If falling in love, if that rush of hormones is the basis for getting married, it explains why so many are doomed to fail. Among my American friends around my age, five of them have already divorced and are on their second marriages. The reason they give for divorcing is that they were not happy. I once talked about this with an American friend of mine who was considering divorce. I explained that the Chinese way was different. We just get married and make it work.

My personal view is that I don't believe love is a prerequisite for a successful marriage. If the two people fall in love, fine. If they never love each other, that doesn't mean they should break up the family. Doc and I have been together for more than thirty years. I was lucky because not too long after I got married, I discovered that I loved him.

And I still do.

YOU CAN GO BACK AGAIN, BUT IT'S NOT HOME

I suspect most kids and teens strive to fit in, even those going through loner phases wearing all black and listening to bleak music. While standing out from the crowd may be a good thing as an adult, when you're young it can put a target on your back. If you're overweight, if you're tall and gangly, if you have a stutter, if you have braces, if you have acne, if your ethnicity is different. Bullying—from verbal taunting to more physical acting out—doesn't need much of a trigger.

While Pat, Annie, and Mary all grew up in areas with larger populations of Taiwanese and other Asian immigrants, I grew up in the Deep South, surrounded by blacks and whites but no other Asians. You'd think that might have created a situation ripe for racial prejudice. But I was lucky. Instead of being the object of scorn or derision, for some reason I was considered exotic, not threatening. In fourth grade there was one boy who was always trying to touch my bone-straight, long hair. After a while I found it annoying. My teacher suggested he was only doing it because he liked me. In retrospect, I think he was just curious because I looked so different from the other girls in class in appearance and dress.

Because of my short stature, many classmates called me Shrimp. But I didn't take it as an insult. I thought it was cute, not to mention accurate. It wasn't an ugly name, and truth be told I liked the attention—not everyone was given a nickname. Sometimes a few of my classmates would jump up and down and pretend to do karate. A stereotype? Of course. But not a negative one. Again, I took it as them trying to connect with me, find some common ground. It felt good-natured, not angry or dangerous. I got along with everyone.

The current atmosphere toward immigrants in some quarters is so different than what I experienced growing up. Perhaps because I grew up in poor neighborhoods where people were disenfranchised because of poverty and lack of opportunity, the fact I was born in Taiwan didn't seem like it was an issue back then. There was no hostility. Life was hard enough for everyone in the projects, so whether born in the United States or elsewhere, we shared the common bond of trying to overcome our shared circumstances; I can't imagine how difficult it must be for people now who face animosity based solely on the fact you weren't born here.

My childhood experiences were my introduction to what I've come to call the China doll effect. Rather than face resentment, I was treated like a curio and often given special treatment, such as having other kids be very protective of me, especially my friend Janine who called herself my bodyguard. Or the kids of my babysitters taking me under their wings.

It continued into adulthood, with people apparently intrigued by how my appearance—short, petite, Taiwanese—is contradicted by my distinct Southern accent and upbeat personality. The stereotype of Asian women is demure, soft-spoken, deferential, and almost fragile—so not me. Whatever the reason, I have often enjoyed preferential treatment for no apparent reason.

In January 2016 Doc and I attended Sundance because I'm interested in independent films, hoping perhaps to one day have one of my books made into a film. We were nobodies with general admission tickets. But it seemed every night we were seated very close to the stage in prime house seats usually reserved for the press or VIPs.

At one point Doc looked at me and shook his head. "You're right. People really do give you the royal treatment," which continued for the five days that we were there.

I thought of my China doll experiences quite a bit when I went back to Taiwan in January 2015, thirty-nine years after our family trip in 1976. Just as when I was ten, it was a strange sensation to be someplace where I wasn't the unique, exotic one. In Taiwan, I was the norm and blended into the crowds anonymously. It was a jolt to my emotional equilibrium. Being different, being unique informed my identity. Even though I was born in Taiwan, I wasn't coming back home, that was the United States. But it was my family's homeland, so I wanted to understand that part of our history, which had so impacted the people my parents became, and by extension, had affected my upbringing.

I made the trip to Taiwan primarily to visit my

son Barrington who was spending a year teaching as a Fulbright grantee in some small, remote village and to attend the Fulbright mid-year conference where they make presentations. But while there I also wanted to explore a bit and learn more about the country.

I flew into what was once Chiang Kai-shek International Airport, now renamed Taiwan Taoyuan International Airport. I could still speak serviceable Taiwanese and asked some airport workers why the name was changed. They all said essentially the same thing: The old name stirred up too many bad feelings. So in 2006 the former general's name was removed.

I spent five days visiting my son, who was in Su'ao, a small city of about 40,000 residents on the northeastern coast of Taiwan, which is known for its volcano-created cold springs and seafood. For much of its existence, Su'ao was a small fishing port located at the base of nearby mountains, but it was developed into an international deep-water commercial port in the late 1970s to take advantage of its natural harbor. Like many cities in the country, development can be spotty, so you could find a four-star hotel and dilapidated homes on the same block.

Wanting to get a feel for the flavor of the area, I did a lot of walking. Even though I blended in by appearance, either because of my clothes or bearing, I obviously wasn't a local, but nobody paid much attention to me. On one of the days I saw a small Taiwanese version of a convenience store except no Big Gulp there. It was like stepping into a time capsule from the 1970s. This store's main product seemed to be lots of American and Chinese cigarette brands. They also sold cans of Starfish tuna; a large selection of liquor, and shelves of candy bars—some brands I hadn't seen in the United States in decades—and other sweets. It was a wonder anyone in town still had teeth.

As I was musing about the local dentition, I heard a sound from my childhood visit to Taiwan that I had never forgotten: cymbals and suonas. I hurried out of the store to watch the funeral procession pass by. About a dozen people were marching, and as they passed I walked behind for a few paces, just to pay respects. It made me feel oddly connected to all the ancestors I had never met who for countless centuries had ended their time on Earth with such a procession. Even though I would have loved to take some photos, it would have been disrespectful, but it will remain a vivid memory until the end of my own days.

As they say, when in Rome, so in the evenings I headed for the night markets, which are a major fixture in the island's nightlife because Taiwanese people love to shop and eat. Some of the markets are dedicated to clothes and trinkets, but the markets are best known for their food stands. A lot of the food would seem familiar to Americans such as gua bao buns, boba tea, braised pork rice, and beef noodles. Other food less so. If you're adventurous you can try the oyster omelet, milkfish, bubble tea (which is really a kind of tapioca), or stinky tofu. Taiwan's answer to blue cheese. A favorite among American tourists is the popcorn chicken, which is fried chicken cut into bite-sized cubes. For me, the markets were definitely a highlight of my time in Su'ao.

In addition to visiting my son and attending the Fulbright presentation, I had set aside the last two days of my trip to take a historical tour with my own guide, arranged by the travel agent. I didn't want to go on a group sightseeing tour; I wanted a more personalized experience to see the Chiang Kai-shek Memorial and learn about life in Taiwan under the dictator and his KMT henchmen.

I met my private tour guide in Taipei. He seemed enthusiastic to be my personal docent and admitted such private historical tours were rare. By my American-accented Taiwanese, he knew I had not grown up on the island, so I gave him the *Reader's Digest* version of my background, including that my parents were staunchly anti-KMT, letting him know I wanted the unvarnished history. In truth, I already had a basic knowledge of Chiang Kai-shek's politics and the cruelties of his regime, but to see places in person where events happened brought them to life and made them more real. Perhaps the most fascinating part of my history lesson was learning about Madame Chiang Kai-shek. My parents never really mentioned her, but as my guide explained, she was an important figure in both the Nationalists' efforts against the communists during the Japanese invasion, and her husband's takeover of Taiwan after World War II.

Hearing the guide describe Madame Chiang, the visual image was a Chinese mashup of Evita Peron and Marie Antoinette. Born into wealth and prestige in either 1888 or 1887 depending on what major news organization you read, she became a prominent political figure in promoting her husband's agenda but in the end became out of touch with the average citizen; as her addiction to power increased so did her ruthlessness to keep it. As the New York Times noted, when Chiang Kai-shek was exiled after the communists seized power in China, she presented herself "as the grand dame of Nationalist politics for many years." She eventually became as feared as her husband, but at one point she was one of the most admired women in the world.

Madame Chiang was born into a well-known wealthy Chinese family (think: the Bushes). The Soongs were influential in both politics and finance, but Soong Mei-ling was most notable because of her American connections. Mei-ling was educated in the United States from 1908 to 1917, beginning in Georgia. By the time she graduated from Wellesley College, she was completely Americanized. After marrying Chiang Kai-shek in 1927 during an opulent ceremony held in Shanghai, she introduced him to Western culture. She taught him to call her darling—one of the few English words he learned—and served as his interpreter, often adding in her own views. The new Madame Chiang used her contacts in the United States to promote his nationalist, anti-communist cause. In 1934 the Chiangs founded the New Life Movement, an initiative to stop the spread of communism by teaching traditional Chinese values. Remember, during this time Taiwan was occupied by Imperial Japan, so communism was the least of its worries.

During World War II Madame Chiang wrote many articles about China that were published in American newspapers and journals. During a 1943 visit to the United States, she became the first Chinese national and just the second woman to address a joint session of Congress. The guide explained that Madame Chiang spoke fluent English but with a Southern accent—that took me aback a bit— from her days as a schoolgirl in Georgia. She was seeking increased American support for China's war against Japan and succeeded in convincing Congress to appropriate millions in financial aid. She was invited to stay at the White House. She accepted but brought her own silk sheets to use.

Considering the United States was fighting Japan in the Pacific made her request a rather easy sell. But Madame Chiang's impassioned speech also captured the public's imagination and generated private donations from Americans who were smitten by her beauty and charisma. For more than twenty years after her historic appearance before Congress, she was a mainstay on the United States' annual list of the ten most admired women in the world.

It can be argued that Madame Chiang was the Nationalist Government's most important diplomat in its efforts to defeat the communist movement. But while propaganda painted the nationalists as noble Chinese battling dangerous communist despots and Japan's evil empire, her husband's political party had plenty of blood on its hands as well. It is now well-documented how many political opponents and critics Chiang Kai-shek murdered in his efforts to win and then keep power both in China and in Taiwan. And it's also known that the Chiangs stole hundreds of millions of dollars of American aid intended for the war effort.

Despite Madame Chiang's long-lasting popularity with the American public, even during World War II many in the American government, including President Franklin Roosevelt, had reservations about the Chiangs amid ongoing reports of their brutality and corruption.

In a memo sent about General Chiang, longtime foreign service officer in China, John Service, warned: "He has achieved and maintained his position in China by his supreme skill in balancing man against man and group against group, and his adroitness as a military politician rather than as a military commander, and by reliance on a gangster secret police."

Madame Chiang also raised concerns. She was attending a dinner at the White House when someone asked how the Chinese government would handle a strike by coal miners. Madame Chiang silently drew a sharp fingernail across her neck, shocking First Lady Eleanor Roosevelt, who later commented, "She can talk beautifully about democracy, but she does not know how to live democracy."

Madame Chiang also wasn't above using her female wiles to promote her husband's causes. According to one story, recounted years later by author Jonathan Fenby, she accompanied her husband to meet Churchill and Roosevelt at a war summit in Cairo in November 1942. "Instead of visiting the pyramids, as Churchill wanted her to do, she walked into the conference chamber, wearing a black satin dress with a yellow chrysanthemum pattern, the skirt slit up the side. Since the general spoke no English, she took over on the Chinese side, constantly correcting the interpreters and setting policy as she chain-smoked British cigarettes." At one point she caused a notable reaction from the men in the room when she shifted position and showed off her legs through the slit in her skirt.

After relocating to Taiwan, Madame Chiang and her husband both blamed the United States for the Nationalists losing China to the communists and pressed Congress to help them reclaim the Mainland. That never happened although the United States supported Taiwan in its efforts to resist being overtaken by Communist China. That was one of the reasons Washington took thirty years to recognize Beijing as the capital of China after the communists seized power.

Despite her efforts on behalf of her husband, their marriage was apparently volatile. She told at least one American politician that she and the general had a sexless marriage, and rumor has it she had a fling with Wendell Willkie, who had run against, and lost to, Franklin Roosevelt for president in 1940. Supposedly, after discovering the general was having an affair with his nurse,

Madame Chiang threw a vase at him and injured him sufficiently that he couldn't go out in public for a while. There was also no love lost between Madame Chiang and General Chiang's son from his first marriage. Madame Chiang never had children so that stepson, Chiang Ching-kuo, became Taiwan's leader when Chiang Kai-shek died in 1975. Shortly after, she moved to New York, where she mostly stayed out of public life, living quietly in an apartment near Gracie Square protected by a squad of bodyguards.

She resurfaced in 1988—by then she was ninety—after her stepson's death, seeking to block Lee Teng-hui from succeeding him as chairman. Her efforts failed, but it sparked a brief revival of interest in Madame Chiang. She credited her longevity on her Christian faith—no word on how she had rectified that with tacitly condoning the murder of thousands of political opponents and stealing millions of foreign aid—and in an article published around her 101st birthday, she said she stayed mentally sharp by reading the Bible and the *New York Times* every day. She died in 2003 at the age of 106—or 105. Either way, she lived a very long, infamous life.

力

I spent the better part of two days learning about Chiang Kai-shek and Madame Chiang and the influence they had on Taiwan.

As I said, the brutality of his regime, especially 228, had been related to me since childhood, but standing on the streets where it happened brought it to life in a visceral way. I imagine it's like going to Gettysburg; one thing to have read Lincoln's address in books, another to read it while standing on the battleground where so many thousands died.

For half a century before the Kuomintang invaded Taiwan, the island had been a modern, industrialized Japanese colony at a time when China was mostly a poor, primarily agricultural country. Yes, there were downsides: you had to speak Japanese, and there was no self-rule. But there was prosperity. The Japanese surrendered to the Allies in 1945, and the Taiwanese people had looked forward to autonomy and democracy. Instead they were overrun by KMT who quickly showed they considered Taiwanese second-class citizens, beginning with the February 28 massacre in 1947.

A reporter from the *New York Times* wrote: "An American who had just arrived in China from [Taipei] said that troops from the mainland arrived there March 7 and indulged in three days of indiscriminate killing and looting. For a time, everyone seen on the streets was shot at, homes were broken into and occupants killed. In the poorer sections the streets were said to have been littered with dead."

At that formative moment many Taiwanese citizens realized despite sharing the same ethnicity, the KMT—and by extension, the Chiangs—were the enemy. And the killing went on for decades. I heard one story about how on the anniversary of 228 in 1980, the mother and twin daughters of a democracy activist were stabbed to death by the KMT. Nobody was ever arrested for the crime. People interpreted the killings as a warning to anyone supporting democracy over KMT rule. It would be seven more years before martial law was lifted and opposition parties decriminalized.

Of course, there is another view of General Chiang.

Historically, Taiwan was an agricultural society. But after World War II it lost its protected Japanese markets and the low-interest-rate loans provided even to tenant farmers, so the economy plummeted. After taking over Taiwan, the KMT deported all Japanese nationals and confiscated their land to create public corporations. With a lot of financial aid from the United States, the KMT government implemented a land reform program, which sold public land to tenant farmers but also severely restricted the size of individual land ownership, forcing owners to sell most of their land to the government. Some credit Chiang with using American aid to industrialize the island in the late-1950s, leading to Taiwan's reputation for producing cheap manufactured exports.

My tour included the National Palace Museum, which was the presidential palace—Chiang Kai-shek's last home—in the Taipei City suburb of Waishuangxi. The dictator had stockpiled more than one million imperial treasures from the Forbidden City in Beijing before fleeing to Taiwan. The items were stashed inside wooden sheds near Chongqing, a western Chinese city. Some were stored in caves dug into the surrounding hills, where the temperature was just right to maintain artwork. The story goes that the Chiangs genuinely believed they would one day go back to rule China and make their re-entrance with these national treasures. Obviously that didn't happen, so Taiwan inherited a palaceful of paintings, calligraphy, jade, porcelain, and other priceless objets d'art that I was very eager to see.

Whether Chiang's goal was to rescue cultural items from Mao Zedong and his Red Guard or to plunder it, the result was the same: the priceless collection found safety in Taiwan. He might have been a reprehensible dictator, but he appreciated art and culture and his actions meant generations of future Taiwanese could enjoy the artistic legacies of the great dynasties.

Art also reflects the society that created it. For example, ceramics from the Tung Dynasty took their color from fruit and other natural sources. Dyes were not available; therefore, ancient pottery and sculptures were not colored as brightly as more recent work. As time went on, artistic creations acquired more detail and more color, co-inciding with improvements in equipment, materials, and rudimentary technology.

At the Shilin Main Presidential Residence in north Taipei, are the original living quarters of Chiang Kai-shek and Madame Chiang where they hosted many dignitaries, including American president Richard Nixon. I was shocked to see he slept in a simple twin-size bed in a spartan room. I admitted to my tour guide that it seemed so primitive, considering the millions he had embezzled. But the guide explained that Chiang's father had died when he was a boy, and his mother was extremely strict and had instilled in him a routine that was precisely regimented and structured. The whole thou shalt not kill and steal bit? Clearly not as much.

I also visited the Chiang Kai-shek Memorial and other historical sites related to the dictator. It occurred to me my parents would banish me if they found out I'd even acknowledged the general's existence like that. Those old scars of oppression ran deep and would never heal. But history explains how we got to where we are today, so I find it endlessly fascinating. I bought so many books at the various gift shops that I had to pay a rather pricey penalty for excess baggage weight on the way home.

I did not spend all my time with the guide, so I did

a lot of exploring on my own as well. I used taxis to get around and would greet each driver in my very limited Mandarin. If they asked me a question I didn't understand, I'd answer in Taiwanese, hoping they knew the language. One cabbie was shocked. Not so much that by my accent and clothing he could tell I was from the United States, but because anyone was speaking Taiwanese.

"That's so obsolete now," he informed me.

Some got downright nostalgic at hearing Taiwanese because very few people on the island born after 1975 know how to speak their country's original language; the KMT effectively wiped it out. But many of the older generations can still speak it, so to them I was like some sort of rare, throw-back gem. I thought it funny that they considered me fluent; just shows how much of a dead language it's become. It seems like such a loss; a native tongue and its inherent idioms and quirks uniquely expresses the personality, mores, and beliefs of a people like no adopted language can.

And just like in the United States, there are regional accents in Taiwan. Ironically, I have a Southern accent there, too. Obviously something I picked up from my father, who came from Nahpee in the south of Taiwan. Apparently my language skills suffered from dated vocabulary as much as diction. A white-haired cabbie who looked to be my father's age told me nobody in northern Taiwan used a word I had—one that meant *townsfolk*—because it was considered provincial.

I had a discussion with another older taxi driver about the White Terror, which is what they call the years under KMT rule. I told him both my parents and I immigrated to the United States in the 1960s.

"I'm so glad your Papa got out. It was horrible here."

He talked about homes burned down, wives and children of activists killed. Massacres large and small. People disappearing. It reinforced just how much these traumatic events had branded the people who had lived through them, how much the fear had never completely gone away. It explained some things about my parents, their paranoia and distrust of authority. Their dismay at my willingness to share my life experiences in books.

It also reinforced just how awful it must have been under the KMT. My parents are not exactly type-A personalities. But living under Chiang's oppressive regime was so bad that they—and the parents of my friends—were willing to move half a world away from their families and the only life they knew. The country they loved—and still did—had become a prison where you could only move forward by accepting oppression. Rather than comply, my father left, and my mother followed. Whatever their reasons, I was grateful because it kept me from having to live and grow up under the kind of fear they had to endure, or worry about those demons impacting the way I raised our sons.

That legacy stopped with me.

EPILOGUE: LOOKING FORWARD

For decades now, Taiwan has been in national limbo. In 1972 Taiwan—officially called the Republic of China (ROC)—lost its seat in the United Nations to the People's Republic of China (PRC), making Taiwan the most populous nation and largest economy that is not a member of the United Nations. In 1979 the US Congress passed the Taiwan Relations Act, which committed the United States to help Taiwan defend itself from attack by Communist China.

Through its One-China Policy, PRC has consistently claimed sovereignty over Taiwan, and Chinese leaders are adamant that the Republic of China is no longer a legitimate country. The Communist China government even refuses diplomatic relations with any country that recognizes Taiwan. As of 2018, seventeen countries and the Vatican maintain official ties with the ROC while other countries maintain unofficial ties through organizations or representatives acting as de facto consulates. Even though Taiwan is self-governing, most international organizations that include Communist China either refuse Taiwan membership outright or only recognize it as a non-state, not wanting retaliation from the PRC.

Despite the deep desire of Taiwanese to determine their own destiny, Communist China has threatened more than once the use of military force in response to any formal declaration of independence by Taiwan, hence decades of living in limbo.

Shortly before he died in 1987, Chiang Kai-shek's son lifted martial law and allowed Taiwanese to visit family on the mainland for the first time since the end of the Chinese Civil War. In 1988 KMT member Lee Teng-hui—sometimes called the father of Taiwan's democracy—became the ROC's first Taiwan-born president, holding the office for twelve years. Under his leadership the ban on opposition parties was rescinded, enabling the pro-independence Democratic Progressive Party (DPP) to compete with KMT candidates in local and national elections. Lee's government also recognized the PRC's control over the mainland and declared that the ROC government represented just the people of Taiwan and its offshore islands of Penghu, Jinmen, and Mazu. Lee's administration also campaigned for Taiwan to regain its seat in the United Nations and other international organizations.

According to ThoughtCo's "A Brief History of Taiwan," in the 1990s, "the ROC government maintained an official commitment to Taiwan's eventual unification with the mainland, but declared that in the current stage the PRC and ROC were independent sovereign states. The Taipei government also made democratization in mainland China a condition for future unification talks.

"The number of people in Taiwan who viewed themselves as *Taiwanese* rather than *Chinese* rose dramatically during the 1990s, and a growing minority advocated eventual independence for the island."

In 1996 Taiwan held its first democratic presidential election, voting Lee Teng-hui back in as president of the KMT.

Making sure the Taiwanese people didn't get too

excited about getting to vote, Communist China fired missiles into the Taiwan Strait. The warning was pretty obvious: pursue true independence at your peril. Upholding the 1979 agreement, the United States sent two aircraft carriers to the area with an equally unambiguous statement: We will defend Taiwan against Chinese aggression.

In 2000 the first Democratic Progressive Party president, Chen Shui-bian, was elected and served for eight years. During that time relations between Taiwan and China were testy. Chen's administration adopted policies that stressed Taiwan's political independence from China but was unable to replace the 1947 ROC constitution in order to apply for United Nations membership under Taiwan. So technically, the ROC's constitution still maintains it holds sovereignty over the mainland, a relic from Chiang Kai-shek's defeat by the communists.

Concerned that the independence movement was gaining traction, the Beijing government passed the Anti-Secession Law in 2005 permitting the use of force against Taiwan to prevent its legal separation from the mainland. Obviously, they had been threatening this for decades but made their "right" a law. The fear of being blown out of the ocean helped the KMT regain the presidency power in 2008.

I should note here that while this was the same nationalist party that murdered on behalf of Chiang Kai-shek back in the day, they were trying to present themselves as now mainstream. For many Taiwanese the jury is still out on that one.

Although tensions eased during Ma Ying-jeou's time in office, with increased trade between the ROC and PRC along with opening Taiwan to tourism from mainland China, among the populace there is no increased support for unification. The vast majority of Taiwanese still dream of true independence and recognition from China that the island is a sovereign nation. Today ex-pat organizations like the European Federation of Taiwanese Associations or the Formosan Association for Public Affairs work to promote Taiwanese independence in Europe and the United States.

China has responded with its own campaign to essentially erase Taiwan's international identity. A 2018 *New York Times* report stated:

> China continues to peel away the dwindling number of allies that recognize Taiwan as an independent country — most recently, on Thursday, Burkina Faso. This week, it blocked Taiwan's representatives — even its journalists — from participating, with observer status, in the World Health Organization's annual assembly in Geneva.
>
> Although China has long sought to isolate Taiwan, people here said its latest efforts have been the most intense in decades. China's economic and diplomatic moves have coincided with a series of military exercises that officials said were explicitly aimed at Taiwan and its president since 2016, Tsai Ing-wen, whose Democratic Progressive Party has traditionally supported independence.

But such aggression seems to only be deepening Taiwanese resolve to one day be independent, as reflected by Democratic Progressive Party candidate Tsai Ing-wen's landslide victory for president. Whether she can lead Taiwan to its long-desired independence remains to be seen.

Author Shawna Yang Ryan observed, "Once, Taiwan identity was something divisive and politicized, but today I think Taiwanese people recognize that it expresses the shared experiences of the people of Taiwan and encompasses the many forces and influences that have led to modern Taiwan."

Those of us who grew up in the long shadow of the White Terror share the dream that those same forces and influences that so impacted our childhoods with fear, will now inspire the next generation of Taiwanese to strive for freedom and self-determination so they can pass on a new legacy, one informed by hope, optimism, and endless possibility.

BIBLIOGRAPHY

Faison, Seth. "Madame Chiang, 105, Chinese Leader's Widow, Dies." *New York Times*, October 24, 2003. https://www.nytimes.com/2003/10/24/world/madame-chiang-105-chinese-leader-s-widow-dies.html.

Fenby, Jonathan. "The Sorceress." *The Guardian*, November 4, 2003. https://www.theguardian.com/world/2003/nov/05/china.jonathanfenby.

Fenby, Jonathan. *Generalissimo: Chiang Kai-shek and the China He Lost.* New York. New York: Simon & Schuster. 2003.

Formosan Association for Public Affairs. http://fapa.org.

Mack, Lauren. "A Brief History of Taiwan." *ThoughtCo.* August 07, 2017. https://www.thoughtco.com/brief-history-of-taiwan-688021.

Mozur, Paul. "Taiwan Families Receive Goodbye Letters Decades after Executions." *New York Times*, Feb 4, 2016. https://www.nytimes.com/2016/02/04/world/asia/taiwan-white-terror-executions.html?rref=collection%2Ftimestopic%2FChiang%20Kai-shek.

Tatlow, Didi Kirsten. "Q&A: Shawna Yang Ryan on the 1947 Incident That Shaped Taiwan's Identity." *New York Times*, January 22, 2016. https://www.nytimes.com/2016/01/23/world/asia/taiwan-shawna-yang-ryan-green-island.html.

Turton, Michael. "Marriage and Women in Taiwan." *The View from Taiwan* (blog). https://michaelturton.blogspot.com/2010/09/marriage-and-women-in-taiwan.html.

Yang, Wen Shan, and Tiffany Liu Ying-ying Tiffany. *Gender Imbalances and the Twisted Marriage Market in Taiwan.* Taipei, Taiwan: Institute of Sociology and Research Center for Social Sciences and Humanities, 2005.

World United Formosans for Independence. http://www.wufi.org.tw/en.

ABOUT THE AUTHOR

CHIUFANG HWANG, MD, is the author of *American Sweetheart, Grown-Up Child,* and *Finding Janine.* She received her doctor of medicine degree from the University of Texas Health Science Center School of Medicine in San Antonio, Texas, and completed her residency in psychiatry and a fellowship in child and adolescent psychiatry at the University of Texas Southwestern Medical School in Dallas, where she lives with her husband and two sons.

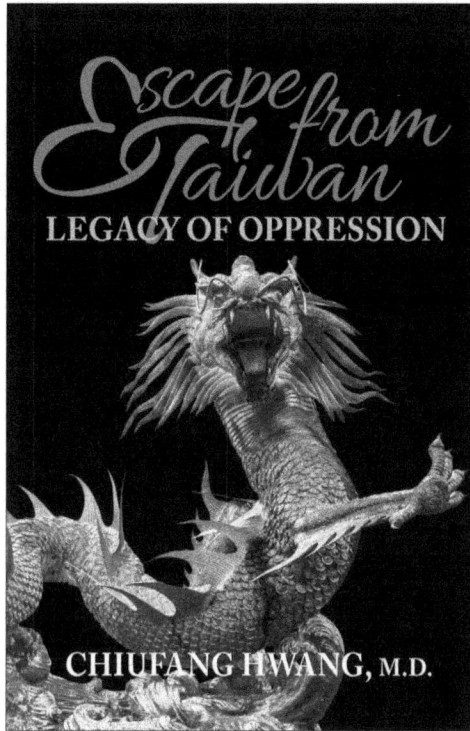

ESCAPE FROM TAIWAN
Legacy of Oppression
CHIUFANG HWANG, M.D.

www.chiufang.com

Publisher: SDP Publishing

Also available in ebook format

Also by Chiufang Hwang, MD:

American Sweetheart: Still *Not Making the Team*

Grown-Up Child: A Memoir

Finding Janine

Available at all major bookstores

 **SDP Publishing**

www.SDPPublishing.com

Contact us at: info@SDPPublishing.com